Silver Profits in
the Eighties

Silver Profits in the Eighties

By
Jerome F. Smith
And
Barbara Kelly Smith

BOOKS IN FOCUS
NEW YORK

First printing........... June, 1982

Second printing .... September, 1982

Third printing........... January, 1983

Manufactured in the United States of America
Library of Congress Catalog Card Number 81-68084
ISBN: 0-916728-56-0

Books in Focus, Inc.
P.O. Box 3481
Grand Central Station
New York, New York 10163

Contents

v

List of Charts

List of Tables

Dear Reader:
Will you please give us your comments on _____

(please write in book name)

Please send me news about your upcoming books on:

☐ all subjects   ☐ money   ☐ politics

☐ survivalism   ☐ philosophy   ☐ other____

Name _____ Address _____

City/State/Zip _____

The following persons may also be interested in your books:

Name _____ Name _____

Address _____ Address _____

City/State/Zip _____ City/State/Zip _____

Foreword

The decade of the 1970s marked the beginning of a revolution in the role of precious metals for investors in the United States. As the real value of traditional investments began to decline in the face of continuing inflation, more and more individual investors became aware of the store of true value in gold, silver and other precious metals.

In a series of landmark books, Jerome Smith identified and explained the historical framework and political basis for today's inflation and the inevitability that it will continue. More importantly, perhaps, he explained clearly and in detail how the individual investor could survive and profit in inflationary times.

This book, *Silver Profits in the Eighties*, is a revised and updated version of Mr. Smith's earlier *Silver Profits in the Seventies*, published in 1972. His earlier book explained in detail the reasons why silver was substantially underpriced at the beginning of the 1970s and why it inevitably had to rise in price throughout the decade. This later book explains how some of the same factors that existed in 1970 continue to exist today and why silver remains one of the most potentially profitable investments for the years to come.

Forecasting prices of any commodity is always hazardous duty. With precious-metal prices being more sensitive to world events than those of other commodities, the job becomes downright perilous. Smith is not a new forecaster on the scene with a few lucky "hits." For over 14 years, he has been predicting the price of silver with incredible accuracy. He has established a record in precious metals unmatched by any other economic forecaster. Clients who followed Smith's recommendation have seen their investment grow many times over.

I believe Smith's success is due to his clear understanding of the nature of human action, the essence of government intervention, and his insatiable desire to seek out all the facts available on the subject at hand.

In the past year, there have been confusing signs of change in the political climate of the United States. A new administration has proposed new methods of fighting inflation and economic stagnation. But the basic causes of our current problems are far too deep-rooted to be overcome in the near term or even over the next decade. Moreover, there is an abundance of historical reason to be skeptical of any government's ability to sustain a disinflationary resolve over an extended period of time. It therefore seems certain that silver will continue to deserve a substantial share of one's investment portfolio over the next decade.

I recommend this book wholeheartedly to every serious investor interested in preserving the real value of his capital and gaining a profit from it.

I'm sure that if you follow the recommendations of Jerome Smith, you will have as much reason as I to be grateful to the man recognized throughout the investment community as the creative force behind contemporary silver investments.

Louis E. Carabini

(Mr. Carabini is founder and President of Monex International, a precious metals firm in Newport Beach, California.)

Preface

If you have the patience to study this review and follow its logic, and if you have some money to invest — it could make you rich. If you are already rich, it can, at least, provide you with a means to keep what you have.

This book is not about what to do with one's complete investment portfolio. There is no discussion of real estate, stocks, bonds, insurance or most other "conventional" investments. It is principally a thorough report about one particular, very exciting, investment, one that I first uncovered nearly two decades ago, when, curiously, I was looking for something else. I was developing a new theory of money[1] and carefully checking my own thinking against the major writings in this field. I wanted to find out, first of all, whether I was possibly making mistakes that someone else had already made, and identified as errors; secondly, whether my "new" ideas were truly original.

The traditional writings on monetary theory that I studied intimately concern the precious metals, gold and silver, because these metals have historically been a central part of money systems and of monetary theory. Through this study, I became interested in the relationship of silver and gold to the world's paper money and in the market outlook for these metals.

Today, silver has many growing and vital uses, production is limited, and existing aboveground supplies are rapidly becoming depleted. Silver prices in 1982 have not yet reflected these factors. For these and other reasons, as I see it, silver prices must move up strongly in the 1983-85 period, and beyond as far as anyone can see. Gold, on the other hand, which has already enjoyed a very substantial rise for monetary

---

[1] A thorough discussion of this theory will be presented in a forthcoming book, tentatively titled *The Separation of Money and State*.

reasons (and will continue to do so as long as present inflationary trends continue), is not so much in demand for non-
monetary use.

Most of the gold that has been mined from the ground is
now stored in the ground — in bank vaults. Industrial demand
for gold today, even though it is growing, is small compared
to current production rates, and is very small compared to existing stocks.

Consequently, within our lifetime, and possibly within this
decade, silver could become more valuable ounce-for-ounce
than gold. Of course, both will become more valuable in
terms of paper money by a large multiple, because of the accelerating and uncontrollable worldwide paper-money inflation that lies ahead.

In the pages that follow, we, my wife and co-worker Barbara and I, pass on to you the results of a jointly undertaken
six-month re-study of this fascinating metal and the many interesting forces that bear upon its increasing value and
underlie its sometimes dramatic price movements.

—Jerome F. Smith

Introduction

Silver is a unique substance. The dictionary describes it as a "white metallic element, sonorous, ductile, very malleable and capable of a high degree of polish. It also has the highest thermal and electrical conductivity of any substance." These and other unique qualities are important for silver's many and varied uses today.

Silver was one of the earliest metals known to man. The richest ores, including much native silver, originally lay right on the surface of the earth. Prior to the last century, some deposits could actually be found glistening in the sunlight (before men burned enough fossil fuels to pollute the air with sulfur). As long ago as 4000 B.C., silver was fashioned into ornaments, some of which were placed in the royal tombs of Chaldea; it was also the favorite ornamental metal for the ancient Mesopotamians, Egyptians, Chinese, Persians and Greeks.

Silver has served as money in more times and in more places than gold. Since many thousands of years ago, it has been used for making mirrors and table utensils. Today, because of its unusual technical properties, it has many new and vital uses, especially in photography, electronics and in the exploding computer and communications industries. It has always been, and is today more than ever, a very unique and useful substance.

Silver is prized today as it has been since pre-historic times because of its beauty, relative scarcity and its resistance to corrosion, properties that have made it useful for both monetary and artistic purposes. In more recent years these applications have been surpassed in importance by industrial uses for the metal based on such outstanding physical and chemical properties as electrical conductivity, light reflectivity and the sensitivity of certain silver salts to light.

The traditional and better-known uses of silver in coinage, tableware and decorative objects have tended to obscure its larger importance as an essential industrial commodity. Today, while silver continues its role as a monetary metal, its use in tableware is diminishing. Future growth of silver as an indispensable resource lies in the industrial field. And here, several trends are converging that predictably will cause a surge in silver's price during the next few years.

Truly outstanding investment opportunities occur only occasionally. In general, the better they are, the rarer they are. Such opportunities are normally long term in their maturation, and by careful study can be foreseen long before they come to the attention of most investors.

When such opportunities do appear on the horizon they are often due to one or more of the following categories of primary causes:

1. Major technological advances creating new products and new demands for particular raw materials, or the lowering of the cost of production for existing products.
2. Market demand that is insensitive (or "inelastic") to changes in price.
3. Market supply that is insensitive to changes in price.
4. Imposition or removal of political intervention in the market.

The very highest profit potentials occur whenever there is a convergence of two or more of these primary causes. Such it is with silver today.

Let's briefly review some highlights of the silver situation with these four factors in mind.

1. Since the beginning of World War II the electronics industry has exploded with new technology and, with its stepchildren, the computer and communications industries, it promises to continue to grow even more rapidly in the 1980s. So also has the growth in these industry's use of silver exploded, as it will continue to do in the foreseeable future. The same is true of the burgeoning photographic industry, which permeates dozens of other related industries.

2. These soaring demands for silver are *price insensitive*, or *inelastic* (i.e., higher prices do not significantly reduce de-

mand). This is because silver, in most of its industrial applications, is used in such minute amounts per unit of end-product that, even though it is a precious metal, the silver cost per unit manufactured is very small as a percentage of unit selling prices, so the small unit cost increase can easily be passed on in the price. And silver is essential to the production of many varied and high volume products (e.g., silverplated switch contacts) for which markets are rapidly growing.

3. While demands for silver are soaring, market supplies are declining, with the trend of new production virtually flat. At the same time that demand is inelastic, *mine production supply is also inelastic.* This is because about 75 percent of the silver produced comes as a by-product of the production of other metals. Silver production has been far less than consumption; it lags by over 100 million ounces each year and cannot be much increased, and for reasons we will explore later, may even decline! In fact, it has already declined compared with earlier peak production periods. The production of silver is very sensitive on the downside to depressions, and only sensitive on the upside to hyperinflationary expectations and/or wars that multiply the price.

4. At the beginning of the 1960s the U.S. Treasury had a huge two-billion-ounce stock of silver. It used half of this for its own coinage—as much as it had used for coin in its entire history prior to the '60s! It sold the other half over the decade at an average rate of 100 million ounces per year—supplying the entire world with enough silver, at increasing prices, to fill the gap between production and consumption, both in the 1960s and the 1970s. Now it is virtually gone.

Thus, *all four of the primary causes* we listed for rare profit opportunities are converging, and soon will be at work simultaneously in the world silver market.

Fundamentally, the outlook for silver is more bullish from 1982 on than for any other commodity I know of—including the much-ballyhooed strategic metals. Silver in 1982 is a cheap precious metal on the way to becoming a scarce and expensive strategic precious metal within this decade.

Ten years ago, when I wrote the results of a five-year study of silver in a book that has since been widely regarded as "the bible" on silver, I said that in the coming decade "silver would double in price and then double again."[1] Only a few of the many who read that in the early 1970s believed me. And, I was wrong. Instead of doubling twice, it doubled three times over on an annual average price basis.

Today, near the tail end of a two-year bear market in the most recent five-year cycle, silver, near $10, is six times higher than ten years ago. Today, it's depressed, it's on the bargain counter and it's poised for a new three-year boom that will take it well over $100 per ounce. For those who buy silver near present levels for long-term gain, it is a truly outstanding investment. I am convinced silver will go far better in the '80s than it did in the 1970s.

In the following chapters we will examine why neither the persistent growth in consumption nor the virtually flat trend in production will be significantly altered, and why (as in the 1970s) silver prices will repeatedly double or treble suddenly (from renewed high double-digit inflation and by sheer force of urgent industrial-demand bidding).

In what follows we will see that silver prices must continue to soar after industrial inventories become depleted ('83 to '85), and why the industrial users must feverishly bid for the little silver that can be offered. And the end is not in sight. A simple extrapolation of existing long-term trends indicates that within our lifetime, silver may very well become more valuable than gold, as it was in ancient Egypt.

----

[1]*Silver Profits in the Seventies* (1972), ERC Publishing Company, West Vancouver, B.C., Canada (out of print).

Silver Profits in
the Eighties

Chapter I

Government Intervention in Silver Markets

In the past, silver was the principal commercial money metal for most of the world's people. This is true from the earliest recording of history, about 6000 B.C., until the 19th century. Prior to the 1870s silver was almost wholly a monetary metal.[1] Relatively small amounts were used in industry. Through most of the last century all major trading nations were on a bi-metallic monetary system and used both silver and gold as money—in bar form as backing for paper money and in intrinsic-value coins. The official mints of Europe, Asia and America all accepted silver by weight at its full monetary value and freely coined the silver metal brought to them by individuals into the coin of the realm, returning about 99 percent of the weight in official coin of certified weight and fineness.

Thus, the price of silver for most of the 19th century was fixed at the coinage value, $1.29 or equivalent per ounce. (Each silver dollar contained .77 ounces of silver.) However, with enormously increasing silver production, especially after 1860 in the Western Hemisphere, world mints became flooded with silver, and there was an over-abundance of silver coins in circulation. Silver was officially overvalued (in terms of gold)—there was simply too much silver being produced. Consequently, the United States and nearly all European nations suspended free coinage of silver in the 1870s. Most nations abandoned bi-metallism and officially adopted the gold standard.

---

[1]See Appendix A for a discussion of "The Long History of Silver Money."

The Early Silver Purchase Acts

The free coinage of silver had effectively been a price control on paper money, fixing the value of the dollar at .77 ounces. With the end of a bi-metallic standard, agitation began for a price control on silver — to try to keep it from falling much below its monetary value ($1.29). In 1878 Western mining-state senators pushed through the Bland-Allison Silver Purchase Act as a subsidy to their constituents, requiring the U.S. Treasury to purchase $4 million in domestic silver per month, to be coined into silver dollars. As a result, the nation was literally flooded with "cartwheels" for the next 12 years. This expansion of the money supply was a unique form of inflation, with the added purchasing power going to Western mining interests (rather than to the government).

In order to appear to be solving the problem, and still have the icing from their cake, the Western senators replaced the Bland Act in 1890 with the Sherman Silver Purchase Act, which upped the purchase amount to $4.5 million per month but relieved the Treasury of the coinage requirement. Instead, it was allowed to store the silver and pay with paper silver certificates, and, as Gresham's Law requires,[2] the paper displaced the coins, and the real dollars (cartwheels) disappeared from circulation. In spite of these efforts, silver market prices fell to under half their former level by the turn of the century, and hundreds of mines that had been profitable at prices near $1.29 were forced to shut down. By 1902, silver's price had dropped to 47 cents per ounce.

After 1900 and before World War I, silver prices, production and consumption were all stagnant at low levels. The onset of World War I brought some dramatic changes, for a few years at least. Two primary factors were involved: (1) The worldwide currency depreciations (paper-money inflations) to finance the war efforts roughly doubled commodity prices; (2) The world's political leaders, obeying Gresham's Law, were distrustful of each others' paper money and required cash specie payment (gold and silver) for war-goods

---

[2]Briefly, Gresham's Law states the truism that bad money (paper) drives good money (precious metal) out of circulation — into hiding.

shipments. The Pittman Silver Purchase Act was passed in 1918, directing the Bureau of the Mint to melt 350 million existing silver dollars and to supply the bullion to Britain (for her to coin into rupees to purchase war materials in India, where British paper was not acceptable). It also authorized the U.S. Treasury to repurchase an equivalent amount of silver in the open market. These purchases were a huge demand factor in world silver markets during that period. Silver prices soared from 75 cents (1917) to $1.02 (1918), stimulating both mine production and speculative demand. As a result, silver prices, the demand for silver and the production of silver, all rose throughout the war years and beyond. In the inflationary rise of commodity prices (about double) following World War I, silver, reacting to both the general price inflation and the massive U.S. Treasury purchases, reached a new high of $1.37 in the speculative fever of the post-war credit boom. With the sharp but short depression of 1921, prices of all commodities plummeted nearly to pre-war levels.

Throughout the first three decades of the 20th century the principal uses for silver were in coinage and silverware. The photographic industry was still in its infancy; the electronics industry was embryonic. Industrial demand was small for the metal and production exceeded consumption.

The Thomas Amendment

The next major development in silver's history came with the deflation, depression, and devaluation of the 1930s. In the absence of any substantial industrial demand at that time, and with the melting of some demonetized European and Asian silver coins, the silver price cascaded from over 50 cents in 1929 to a 1933 low of 25 cents. All commodity prices fell. Once again, as in the 1870s and '90s, a movement arose to halt a prolonged deflationary spiral by restoring currency values to the level at which wartime and post-war debts had been contracted. And once again a political "remedy" was proposed.

The Thomas Amendment to the Agricultural Adjustment Act of 1933 envisioned the printing of more paper money and unlimited coinage of silver. Additionally, it permitted debtor countries to pay U.S. debts in silver valued at 50 cents per ounce—double the then-current market price. Domestic and world prices moved up. Under the London Economic Conference Agreement, the U.S. government agreed to purchase its own entire domestic yearly output of silver (so that American silver supplies wouldn't depress English silver prices). The amendment, in addition, authorized increased open-market purchases of government securities and a reduction in the gold content of the dollar. By Presidential decree (at the request of insolvent bankers) all banks were closed, an embargo was put on gold and the dollar was allowed to float.

The change in the dollar's gold content received the most emphasis in early "New Deal" days. After the dollar had floated for several months, under the authority of the Gold Reserve Act of 1934, its value was officially fixed at 59.06 percent of its formerly established (1900) value in terms of gold.

But much to the surprise of the theorists who influenced the Administration's decision—theorists who posited a close relationship between the price level of commodities and the gold content of the monetary medium—the price level did not automatically respond, in spite of the 41 percent reduction in the gold content of the dollar. Silver inflation was therefore introduced as a supplement to the ineffectual gold inflation—and as an answer to the perennial senatorial demand to "do something for silver."

The downward trend in the price of silver had been interrupted only twice since 1873, during the silver-purchase period around 1890 and again during World War I. After the turn of the century, in fact, the market price rarely exceeded one-half the coinage value. Silver was in a state of monetary confusion most of the time; some was used for subsidiary coins, some circulated in the West in the form of standard silver dollars, and a roughly fixed stock of silver certificates remained in circulation as a relic of the 1890s.

At the end of 1933, with the market price of silver at about 44 cents an ounce—75 percent above the depression low—unlimited U.S. Treasury purchases of newly mined silver at 64 cents an ounce were initiated, under the authority of the Thomas Amendment. Inflationist pressure then injected even further political action, the Silver Purchase Act of 1934. Under its terms, the Secretary of the Treasury was directed to purchase silver at home and abroad until the market price reached the traditional mint price of $1.29 an ounce, or until the monetary value of the U.S. Treasury's silver stock reached one-third of the monetary value of its gold stock. Speculative buying was stimulated. Treasury and private speculative purchases quickly bid prices up to 80 cents. Large speculative profits were made. Then, as now, U.S. Treasury officials were chagrined that speculators were profiting from the (obvious) results of Treasury policies. They felt that such greed should be punished. *The U.S. Treasury issued an edict that taxed domestic silver transactions 50 percent*, to "capture the windfall profits created by the Treasury." The price at which Treasury purchases were made was changed on several different occasions during the ensuing dozen years; originally $0.6464, it was eventually set at $0.9050 in 1946.

Under the authority of the silver-purchase legislation of the 1930s and subsequent presidential proclamations, the U.S. Treasury acquired altogether 3,200 million ounces of silver —nearly half of it from global supplies in the four-year period 1931-37, and the remaining half in the subsequent two decades. *About 110 million ounces consisted of silver that was "nationalized" in mid-1934, when the Administration required domestically held non-monetary silver to be turned in at 50 cents per fine ounce.* (The confiscatory 50 percent tax and actual *physical confiscation* of Commodity Exchange stocks made it impossible for the New York Comex to function. Silver trading had to be shut down completely.) Could this happen again to investors who hold silver in the U.S.? Perhaps it is unlikely, but there is this precedent.

At the beginning of World War II, the U.S. Treasury held a stock of almost 3 billion ounces of silver. As in World War I, political leaders did not trust each other's paper money and demanded specie payment (gold and silver) for war goods. The U.S. required 900 million ounces of silver for international transactions in World War II, compared to the 350 million ounces of silver that were used for such purposes in World War I.[3]

Until 1955, the U.S. Treasury support price for newly mined domestic silver was higher than the market price, so the U.S. government purchased domestic metal at the higher price while U.S. silver-using industries purchased low-priced foreign metal. From 1955 onward, the market price exceeded the support price, and silver users began to purchase supplies from the Treasury as well as from domestic mines.

Chart 1
The Silver Price 1917 Through 1970

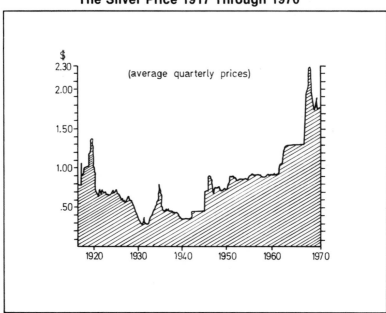

In the preceding quarter-century, the Treasury had purchased $2 billion in silver and sextupled the physical quantity used as currency backing or held in stockpiles. The silver pro-

---

[3]As of late 1981 the U.S. held a "strategic" stockpile of silver of 139.5 million ounces, long reserved for such uses in the event of World War III. However, by legislation passed in July 1981, this silver has been declared surplus and was ordered to be sold by auction bidding over a three-year period.

Chart 2
The Silver Price 1970 Through 1980

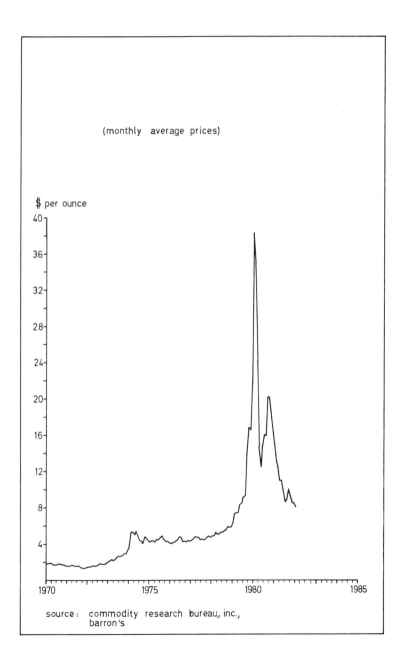

(monthly average prices)

\$ per ounce

source: commodity research bureau, inc.,
barron's

gram during that period failed to achieve either of the objectives specified in the 1934 Silver Purchase Act (a market price equal to the monetary value of $1.29, or a 1-to-3 ratio of the monetary stocks of silver and gold). It did, however, result in the U.S. Treasury entering the critical 1960s with a huge stock of two billion ounces of silver.

The upsurge in world market demand in the early 1960s, both for industry and for coinage, pushed silver prices up through the 91 cent Treasury buying price to its $1.29 selling price. The market thus accomplished quickly what all the laws and edicts of the previous quarter-century had failed to do, and more: it forced the U.S. Treasury to make massive sales from its hoard to hold the price at that level, in a vain attempt to keep U.S. silver coinage circulating.

Long-Range Effects
of Government Price Control

An examination of silver's price history shows that: (1) Whenever government intruded into the silver market, its actions were opposed to the trend of the market; (2) The maximum period of government success in influencing a trend or holding a fixed price was about four years; (3) When the government influence ended, the price always moved in a direction opposite the control.

The explanation for this is simple, so simple that anyone, except those no higher in intelligence than a bureaucrat, can understand it. The explanation is this: When a price trend is down it means that, overall, more of the product is currently coming onto the market than is currently wanted at the earlier (higher) price(s). Therefore a lower price is chosen by sellers as a preferred alternative to making no sale, and is also chosen by buyers as a preferred alternative to making no purchase. At successively lower prices, less and less is produced and sold, while at the same time more and more is wanted and bought. This happens until supply and demand come into an approximate balance at a price that is profitable for a smaller number of producers (the most efficient ones), and that is now profitable for a larger number of consumers (including some new ones who couldn't afford the product at the higher prices). Everyone has what he wants; everyone is happy.

When a price trend is up *or* down and a government interferes, the market process is temporarily put into reverse. Overabundant supplies become more overabundant, and scarce supplies become more scarce . . . until the imbalances become so enormous (and sellers and buyers alike become so unhappy) that finally, in spite of all the apparent power that *any* government has ever had, the market ultimately always has its way.

The longer and greater the interference, the more sudden and precipitous the market reaction will be. All the more quickly, prices will move all the lower or all the higher — *opposite the direction of the control* — to bring the demand made and the supply offered in the market into balance, and to reduce or increase the production level *and* the consumption rate to maximize the profits (and happiness) of both sellers and buyers.

Government interference in markets, on balance, *always* produces price distortion, misallocation of capital resources, inefficiency, mal-production, mal-consumption and unhappiness for both producers and consumers.

Since the 1960s, when the U.S. government's silver supplies were virtually dissipated, government intervention into the silver markets via manipulation of silver supplies has been impossible. And we predict that the announced sale over the next three years of 105 million ounces of the strategic stockpile — if indeed this silver is sold — will have little or no effect on the market when set against the burgeoning demand for the metal.

CHAPTER II

Private Intervention in Silver Markets

With the U.S. Treasury virtually out of the supply picture after 1971, the impact on the markets of the absence of this previously dominant supplier was bound to have a corresponding bullish impact on silver prices in the future. And it did. The annual average silver price, under $2.00 per ounce in 1970, '71 and '72, moved erratically upward as follows: 1973: $2.56; 1974: $4.71; 1975: $4.42; 1976: $4.35; 1977: $4.62; 1978: $5.40; more than doubled in 1979 to $11.09 and almost doubled again in 1980 to an annual average price of $20.70.

In January 1980 silver peaked at a price of $48.80; two months later, the price had plummeted to $10.80. Through the remainder of 1980 and 1981, silver stayed at around the $10 level. In the market debacle of early 1980 thousands of investors lost fortunes large and small. For many, silver was utterly discredited as an investment, even though nothing had happened (or has happened since) to alter its supply and demand fundamentals. Many more blamed the Hunts for cornering the market and artificially driving up the price; yet they lost more than perhaps anyone else.

Yet the real culprit was not silver itself, nor the Hunts — nor even, in this case, the government except in an indirect way. The culprits were the officials of the commodity exchanges where silver futures are traded, whose unwarranted intrusions into the markets caused the price of silver first to soar to unreasonable (for that time) heights and subsequently to plummet to unwarranted depths.

It is distressing, after a century of U.S. government intervention in silver markets, that government-sanctioned ex-

13

change officials would begin the first decade of free silver markets with a series of arbitrary and self-serving private interventions. Their rule changes were designed to shift their own massive paper losses from short positions into massive realized gains for themselves and massive losses for the silver trading public. They succeeded in this with legal impunity (so far, at least) but they also virtually destroyed their own market and—because of the public's loss of confidence in the integrity of market institutions—they depressed both the public appetite for participation in silver markets and the silver price for two years—far longer, no doubt, than they intended.

Because of the magnitude and length of the impact of these officials' interventions, we include within this chapter a brief account of them ahead of the more fundamental analysis of silver that we take up in Chapters III through V.

The Onset of the 1980 Bull Market

. . .Each metals exchange is presided over by a board of directors that makes and can change rules to prevent trade members from getting financially buried by speculators who have not invested in exchange seats. Juvenal once asked, "Who will guard the guards?" In the case of commodities futures exchanges dominated by trade and floor interests, the rules are made by the guards to guard the guards.[1]

Early in 1978 when the silver price was about $5 per ounce, the Commodity Exchange of New York (Comex) set a $1,000 minimum margin—the amount a customer had to deposit in cash with his broker for a 5,000-ounce contract, or a short silver position. The daily limit or maximum move up or down from the previous day's settlement was twenty cents an ounce, or $1,000 per contract. Late in 1978, as the price of silver moved up to the $6 range, Comex officials raised the mini-

---

[1]Paul Sarnoff, *Silver Bulls* (1980: Arlington House Publishers, Westport, Connecticut; pp. 72, 73).

mum margin to $2,000. So far, so good. The officials were acting properly. The hanky-panky began in 1979.

On September 4, 1979, at a Comex board meeting, Dr. Henry Jarecki, a Mocatta Metals Company principal and a board member, is said to have suggested that silver margins be raised to $3,000 a contract, and daily trading limits doubled from twenty to forty cents.[2] The board so ruled.

Two days later, when the September contract had moved from $11.02 to $11.80 an ounce, the doctor again suggested to the board that margins should be raised, this time to $5,000 and that variable trading limits be adopted. The board agreed. Dr. Jarecki, it should be noted, was reported to be heavily short in the silver market at the time.[3] These suggestions were embraced by his fellow board members, most of whom were no doubt also on the short side. In the absence of overriding opposing forces these changes would discourage new long buyers, encourage new short position-takers and tend therefore to push prices down. In spite of this tendency however, silver futures very shortly thereafter underwent eight days of limit-up trading and three days of lower-than-limit moves.

One well-publicized major bullish influence at the time, of course, was the ongoing heavy buying by the Hunt brothers. In October and November of 1979 the price moved very little around $16 per ounce as the Hunts and others kept buying in spite of the increased margin requirements, while other less well-heeled traders were driven away.

Since 1974 the Hunts had maintained sizable silver futures positions running to thousands of contracts in both Chicago and New York, and for five years they had rolled over these futures into more distant months as the spot month neared or arrived. And in spite of the board officials' moves they kept right on doing so in September and October 1979.

---

[2]This remark, and much of the specific information in the rest of this chapter, is excerpted from *Silver Bulls*, by Paul Sarnoff.

[3]An investor who is "short" in a futures market holds more contracts for future sales than he does for future purchases—i.e., he expects the price of silver to decline in the future.

Obviously the exchange officials would have to use heavier weapons to drive the Hunts out of their massive holdings of long futures contracts. So, on the morning of October 25 the Chicago Board of Trade (CBOT) board of directors invoked their "temporary emergency powers" (despite there being no emergency), and adopted a self-serving rule setting a limit of six hundred silver futures contracts per account. Prior to this, anyone could go long or go short as many silver contracts as he desired or could afford.

The Comex and CBOT boards were by then obviously determined to make whatever rules were necessary to cause the longs (the outsiders) to let go and to prevent a squeeze on the shorts (the insiders themselves).

Since the margin raises decreed by the exchange boards had all but shut out the small speculators, the open interest on the short side of the two-way trade gradually congested into the thin ranks of the bullion dealers. This occurred by the third week of November 1979.

> On Monday, November 26, spot silver rose by 8.5 cents to $16.405. The open interest for December on November 23 stood at 9,544 contracts, or 47,720,000 ounces. Delivery of all the involved silver in the futures contracts would have required $7.8 billion. By the close of business on November 28, when the value of the spot month settled at $18.26 after a one-day leap of $1.46 per ounce, the open interest in December silver had dropped to 7,515 contracts. By the close of business November 29, when silver for December delivery settled at $18.16, there were only 2,465 contracts open. And on the last trading day of November the December open interest stood at 2,310, a rather small number for any contract month that still had seventeen trading sessions to go before the contract could be wiped off the exchange listing. . .
>
> . . .With a total open interest of 11.5 million ounces, when there were over 55 million ounces sitting in Comex warehouses. . .the Comex board [had been told] back in September, "You don't have a problem."
>
> But evidently some of the board members did. They lost plenty of money on overhedged or naked short positions as the December holders of the longs profited.
>
> By early December practically the entire March '80 open interest on the short side appeared to be held by the bullion dealers, including Mocatta Metals, J. Aron, Philipp Brothers (a division of Engelhard), Sharps, Pixley, etc.[4]

[4]Paul Sarnoff, *Silver Bulls*, pp. 74, 76.

All through December silver surged higher, reaching a new high of $21.65 on December 14th.

On Monday and Tuesday, the seventeenth and eighteenth, silver for December '79 delivery leaped skyward. When the smoke settled by the end of the week on December 21, the price of December silver settled at $24.35.

The March Comex delivery ended the month of December trading with three limit-up sessions, gaining $1 an ounce each day.

Imagine! A future whose former daily limit moves were calculated on a change of 20 cents per ounce now found itself moving daily up $1 an ounce, or five times the former limit. There were more than 30,000 contracts in the March delivery, or 150 million ounces. Every $1 move up meant the bullion dealers who were on the short side had to pony up $150 million a day variation margins to the exchange clearing house.[5]

Squeezing the Longs

According to the press at the time there were two large buying influences in the silver market: the Hunts, their families, and allied corporations; and the "foreign investors," meaning Norton Waltuch (of Conti-Commodity, acting for foreign clients, such as the wealthy Naji Nahas[6]), and other foreign and American investors who did their buying through Swiss banks.

Obviously, if these buyers, along with many others, acted together and in concert with the Hunts, then the longs could dominate the shorts. In that case the supposed concern of the exchanges and the CFTC might have been legitimate. Even more obviously, such numerous, diverse and scattered investors could not possibly have acted in concert. The exchange officials used this stated fear as a "justification" for their unprecedented and unscrupulous manipulation of the silver market from October 1979 onward. Their rule changes were aimed to force the longs to let go of their December '79 and March '80 positions in the fall of 1979. However, persistent

---

[5]*Ibid*, pp. 78, 79.

[6]The Lebanese silver bull from Sao Paolo, Brazil.

Chart 3
Silver Prices, September 1979 Through March 1980

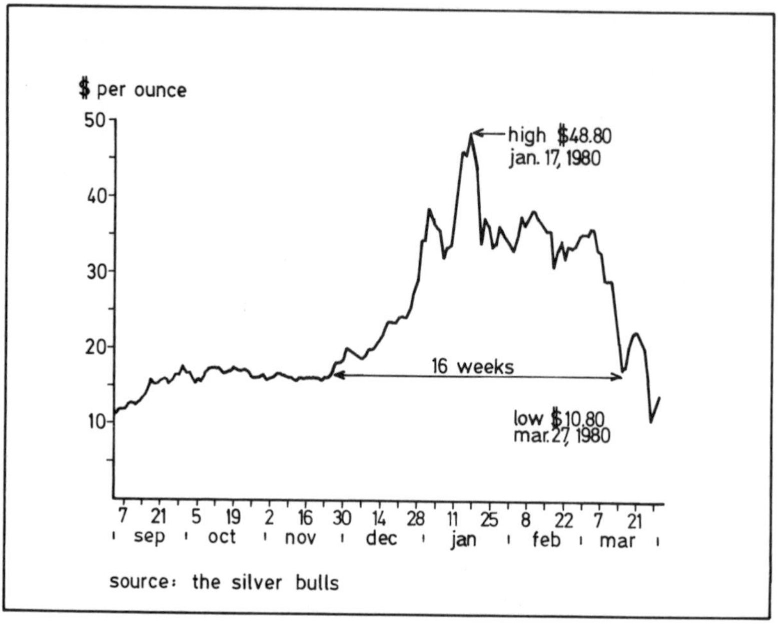

buying by the outsiders caused prices to soar in mid- to late-December 1979 and again early January 1980.

The critical March Comex silver contract ended 1979 at $29.05, almost 50 percent higher than its level at the start of December 1979. A rise of $10 an ounce on 30,000 silver contracts meant the shorts had to put up deposits of at least $1.5 billion. And, by the end of 1979 the increase in equity in the March Comex delivery for the Hunt group hovered well over $1.2 billion.

One effect of the extraordinarily high prices from December 1979 to February 1980 was a scramble by householders for mismatched, worn and unwanted silverware, jewelry — and even family heirlooms—from their bureaus and attics to cart to market. Retail outlets sprang up by the hundreds offering ready cash for old gold and silver scrap, and the coin shops began to do business at a level never before dreamed or imagined. And conversely, another effect was the public's withdrawals of cash from banks to buy precious metals, which caused increasing concern at the Federal Reserve (Fed). Paul Volcker, the Federal Reserve chairman, prepared to act.

Exchange officials were informed that the Fed was concerned because the rising price of silver and the soaring price of gold had a weakening effect on the dollar. The GSA had stopped its Treasury gold auctions after December, so the supply of gold was reduced.

This was the atmosphere when the silver market opened on the London Metal Exchange Wednesday, January 2 and spot silver traded at 1,690 pence. Some five hours later, when trading opened on the Comex in New York, silver shot up the dollar limit to settle at $30.05.

> Would the longs hold out and squeeze the shorts? Mr. Goldschmidt of Conti had assured the Comex directors that it wouldn't happen. The Hunts had given similar assurances in personal visits at the exchanges, at the CFTC, and through letters.
> But the Comex board members who were short were evidently not satisfied with such apodictical assurances. They wanted the longs to let go, and the longs were in no hurry.[7]

By early January, the board officials were in a panic; on January 7, 1980, the special margin committee, chaired by Dr. Jarecki, suggested that the Comex set a limit of 500 on the number of contract positions any one trader by himself or in concert with others could hold in any single delivery month. The Hunts, of course, had many thousands of contracts, and Norton Waltuch and the so-called "foreign investors" also held positions well in excess of the proposed five hundred-contract limit. A "literal" limit of a market total of two thousand contracts in all delivery months was also adopted "in order not to shut down the New York silver market completely." At the same meeting, on January 7, they adopted "Silver Rule 7," making any account with more than a hundred contracts a "reportable account."

---

[7]Paul Sarnoff, *Silver Bulls*, p. 80.

These new rules were clearly designed to force the few remaining large longs to sell most of their holdings on or before the effective date of February 18 and eliminate once and for all any danger of a squeeze on the March delivery.

In the wake of the board's adoption of the restrictive Silver Rule of January 7, the outsider longs began buying January and February silver contracts up to the monthly position limit of five hundred, creating the possibility of a squeeze on the shorts for those months. Upon seeing this, the board members ruled on January 9 that positions in January and February Comex silver be restricted to no more than fifty contracts per account. The die, it appeared, was now cast to force the longs to let go.

Nevertheless, expecting a one-day down market on January 8, and a less than limit-up move of 75 cents on January 9, silver moved limit-up each trading day since the month opened. The bullion dealers who were short had to deposit more than $135 million a day in variation margin—and high interest rates were getting higher.

Simultaneously, a burst of buying had appeared in the London markets. The Hunts and the Saudis apparently were transferring their business from Comex to the LME.

The growing anxiety of the bullion dealers was evident. So was their determination to make the silver tracks run the other way.

In London on January 14, silver traded at 1,810 pence for spot, and then moved higher. By January 18, LME purchases had pulled the spot price to an all-time record of 2,150 pence. In New York on Comex the spot January contract traded at $48.80 on Thursday, January 17, and then dropped slightly to close on Friday at $46.80.

On the next trading day, Monday, January 21, the Comex board held an emergency meeting at 9:00 a.m. on the silver situation.

Someone suggested that the board limit trades to liquidation only, to get the longs to let go. But first the board had to declare whether an emergency situation existed. Even though this was not the case, the Comex board resolved that an emergency existed because of significant concentrations that could cause the March maturity and other maturities to fail to liquidate in a normal fashion.

Therefore, the board postponed opening the market until 11:30 a.m. (Comex silver normally opens for trading at 9:50 a.m.)

The ensuing discussion ran past 11 a.m., and the board further postponed the silver market opening to 12:30 p.m.

Then the board recessed.

When the meeting resumed, the discussion focused on the level of silver margins. The time for the silver opening was moved yet again, to 1:30 p.m.

The Comex attorney then summarized the proceedings, a motion was made, seconded, and carried to make silver trading for liquidation only.

There could be no new buying by anybody, except shorts who were liquidating. The longs had no place to go, no normal market to absorb their holdings. They found themselves now locked in perilously by the Comex rules — rules formulated by a board including at least four members representing firms that held the major portion of the shorts in all the outstanding open interests.

The longs had no one to sell to, except those firms that had open shorts, firms that had helped to make the self-serving Silver Rule 7.

While in London on January 21 silver traded steadily at 2,150 pence for spot metal, the spot month in New York on Comex presented one of the wildest swinging markets ever seen in silver trading. High for the trading session on January 21 in January silver was $49. Low was $37, and the contract closed at $44.

But from that day on the silver price went downhill. The January silver contract went off the boards a few days later at $33.95. On the last trading day in January the March Comex contract settled for $35.70, with 13,060 contracts open.

The first day of February trading activity on Comex found the March silver contract under pressure, supposedly because the longs had no place to go. But evidently they did have plenty of monetary muscle at the time, because they allowed the word to get around that they would not liquidate their positions, but instead would demand delivery and pay in cash.

The restrictive rules might never have resulted in the silver price collapse that came in March if the Federal Reserve had not made waves about banks and their loans to bullion hoarders like the Hunts, and if interest rates had not been twisted up sharply by the Fed.

The government's harsh attitude toward gold and silver loans, together with the effect of credit controls and rising interest rates established to try to control a malignant inflation, put a severe crimp in the plans of the longs to stand for delivery and to finance any silver so delivered.

The holders of the long side of the March Comex silver open interest had little room to maneuver. They could only liquidate through offset — and the accommodating buyers were the trade member shorts.

On Monday, February 19, the spot month (February) on which prices could move without limit dropped $4.80 an ounce to $31.

With the market biased in favor of the shorts, they stood to make millions during the descent that led to Silver Thursday.

During the first week in March the Comex spot month declined about 10 percent from $35.20 to $32.90. But the following week the prime rate rose to 20 percent. President Carter made his pitch about the profligacy of consumers, whom he blamed for inflation the government actually caused. The price of silver collapsed about 30 percent in five trading sessions to stand at $21 an ounce at the end of trading on March 14.[8]

This set the stage for a day that will go down in business history as Silver Thursday, March 27, 1980, when silver plunged to its 1980 low of $10.80.

As of January 1, 1980, the Hunts and their corporate allies controlled over 192 million ounces of silver in physical metal, options, futures contracts, and forward contracts. Their positions were divided as follows:

Nelson Bunker Hunt	79,028,000 ounces
Wm. Herbert Hunt	47,569,000 ounces
IMIC	61,873,000 ounces
Hunt International	774,900 ounces
Planet	3,000,000 ounces
Total	192,244,900 ounces

For every drop of $1 in the price of silver the equity of this massive position declined more than $192 million. And, of course, for every dollar of rise in the silver price the value of the holdings rose $192 million.

In a later Congressional inquiry the Hunts maintained that their silver had cost them less than $10 an ounce, on average; their year-end '79 holdings represented an increase in equity of $2.7 billion.

On March 28, 1980, the day after Silver Thursday, the reduced Hunt silver stockpile stood at near 102 million ounces, and their physicals and LME forward positions through their associated corporations were about 39 million ounces.

If the Hunts, strapped for cash, had been forced to dump this 141 million ounces of silver on the market, there can be little doubt that silver would have dropped below $5 an ounce.

---

[8]*Ibid*, pp. 85, 86, 87, 88, 89, 90, 92.

Silver Thursday created plenty of headlines and pictures of the Fed chairman puffing cigars, and of Congressional committees seeking to find out why silver went from $6 in January 1979 to $50 in January 1980, then cascaded to $10.80 on Silver Thursday before recovering.

More than a year later some of the federal agencies who collaborated, at least tacitly, finally produced a report. Not surprisingly, it

> . . . exonerates commodity exchange officials for their part in allegedly engineering the 1980 silver collapse.
>
> The 500 page study, which was jointly prepared by the Commodity Futures Trading Commission (CFTC); the Securities and Exchange Commission (SEC), the Federal Reserve Board and the Treasury Department, also avoids specifically blaming the Hunt brothers for "cornering the market." But neither does it give them a clean bill of health, the implication being that the government is not through with the Texas billionaires yet. The main purpose of the study is to argue for (what else?) more government regulation of the futures markets.
>
> . . . The report admits that it could find no evidence that the Hunt brothers and several Arab investors were acting in concert to corner the silver market and drive prices up. In fact, it says that the behavior of the Hunts and other interests "were in several respects inconsistent with conduct normally attributable to a market squeeze." . . .
>
> The Hunts are in a battleroyal with the SEC, which has been investigating every aspect of the family's affairs for over a year. The SEC is trying to prove that the Hunts deliberately put banks, brokers and their customers at jeopardy. . . .
>
> Conspicuously absent [from the report] is any restriction on the Boards of Directors of the exchanges, who many believe had vested interests in manipulating the price of silver downward. . . .
>
> It is also likely that silver wouldn't be as low as it is today if the market had been allowed to operate freely. . . .[9]

The Near Death of the Futures Market

When Jerome Smith stated last year [1979] that he believed the U.S. silver futures markets would close down by the end of 1980, many observers were taken aback. And yet the months since then have seen this forecast on its way to becoming fact. Briefly, he believed that the growing shortage of silver would lead to a situation where contracts

---

[9]*Deaknews*, August 1981.

would be outstanding for much more silver than existed in the warehouses. That's exactly what has happened.

The managers of the various exchanges have realized that if the holders of the contracts to buy silver in the future were to proceed to take delivery, the price would surge astronomically. So they have tried to restrict the acquiring of such contracts by repeatedly raising the minimum margin requirements from only $1,000 per contract to a whopping $50,000. Silver's price soared nonetheless, and . . . the two major U.S. futures markets, Comex in New York and the Chicago Board of Trade, made a move which would destroy the futures markets altogether. They banned all new purchases of silver and allowed only for current positions to be liquidated. . . .[10]

A further consequence of the commodity exchange officials' intrusions into the futures markets was that by the end of 1980 investors had virtually deserted the U.S. markets. Some of them took their business to London or Zurich; many simply got out altogether and stayed out through 1980 at least. The daily average volume plunged from 26,872 contracts traded in September 1980 to only 8,466 daily average in December.

Table I paints a very clear picture of the decline in trading in the U.S. silver futures market, especially in the Chicago market (CBOT) where the Board officials' meddling was most extreme: annual volume fell from 2.7 million contracts in 1979 to a mere .34 million in 1980 — a drop of 87 percent. Though they didn't officially shut down, as I had predicted a year earlier, they might as well have done so. Note the dramatic drop in all futures markets' volume from 1979 to 1980.

Table I
Silver Futures Contract Volume
U.S. Exchanges, 1976-81

	Comex	CBOT	Mid-America	Totals
1976	3,741,908	2,011,041	447,513	6,200,462
1977	3,540,047	2,257,059	366,585	6,163,691
1978	3,822,085	2,657,833	378,049	6,857,967
1979	4,080,619	2,720,589	361,576	7,162,784
1980	1,058,734	341,033	209,494	1,609,261
1981	1,240,720	251,191	143,051	1,634,962

Source: Consolidated Gold Fields Limited, *Gold 1981.*

[10]Christopher Weber, *World Market Perspective*, Vol. XIII, No. 2, February 21, 1980.

Judging from the dramatic 1979-80 decline in trading, traditional traders in the U.S. markets were exhibiting their lack of confidence in the management of the U.S. exchanges.

The much-publicized "cornering of the silver market" by the Hunts provided the fuel for government regulatory authorities to raise their collective voice in an attempt to exploit the silver turmoil, as an excuse for more government investigation of and intervention into futures markets. However, emphatic opposition of this viewpoint was taken up almost immediately from "industry spokesmen" — a euphemism for the culpable and vulnerable exchange officials, in our view.

The opposition to more regulatory inquiry and intervention argued that the futures market had worked precisely the way it was supposed to. Silver had obviously been bid up to astronomical heights because of speculative demand and was over-priced as a result. If the officials had kept their influence out of the market, it would have adjusted itself to a level more representative of supply-and-demand factors. In general, the two preceding contentions are correct; however the point is that downward adjustment would have been far more orderly and less steep had the exchange officials not abusively tampered with the markets' operation. The resulting impact of what would otherwise have been a more or less normal correction in the silver price, became a disaster for many hundreds of smaller traders when the exchange officials issued their prohibition on new "buy" orders, yet permitting new "sell" orders to be entered. The resulting precipitous 1980-81 drop in silver prices was therefore assured.

In view of the shambles caused by their intrusions, it seems unlikely that exchange officials will again tamper so destructively with their own markets. And their interventions did at least make it possible for farsighted long-term investors to buy silver for under $10 per ounce in 1981, and (we expect) under $20 per ounce in 1982.

CHAPTER III

The Demand for Silver

Every economic analysis involves a study of three basic factors: (1) Demand; (2) Supply and (3) Price. In a free market, price is the equalizer of the other two factors. However, one must begin with the first two, study each of them separately, then study them together. Only then can one begin to study price levels, price trends and price movements, past or present. Only after the past and present situation of all three factors have been thoroughly explored, can one make an informed judgment about the likely future course of any one, two or all three of the factors involved.

Price movements are where profits are to be made for those who can correctly anticipate them. However, one must begin at the beginning. We will begin with an examination of silver demand and the effects of all known significant determinants or influences on demand.

Before 1940, silver was used primarily for silverware and coins. But in the '40s, industry began consuming larger and larger annual amounts of silver. Industrial consumption increased from about 75 million troy ounces in the early 1940s to 450 million troy ounces in the late 1970s.

According to figures published by Handy & Harman, during the period 1974 through 1980 the United States consumed more silver than any other country in the non-Communist world. During 1979-80 the U.S. accounted for approximately 38 percent of the total non-Communist world consumption. Table II gives a breakdown of U.S. silver consumption by category.

Table II

U.S. Consumption of Silver, 1970-80
(millions of troy ounces)

	1970	1971	1972	1973	1974	1975	1976	1977	1978	1979	1980
Photographic materials	38	36	38	52	50	46	55	54	64	66	49
Electrical and electronic products	32	34	43	44	35	32	36	37	37	38	32
Other Industrial*	18	16	18	27	25	24	26	25	23	22	16
Jewelry, mirrors and sterlingware**	37	38	46	63	45	48	45	34	34	28	18
Medallions and coins***	3	6	6	10	22	7	9	4	3	3	4
Total industrial consumption	128	130	151	196	177	157	171	154	161	157	120
Coinage	1	2	2	7	1	3	1	–	–	–	–
Total consumption	129	132	153	197	178	160	172	154	161	157	120

*Includes bearings, brazing alloys and solders, catalysts, medical and dental and miscellaneous uses.
**Includes electroplated ware.
***Includes commemorative objects.

Source: U.S. Bureau of Mines, Department of the Interior.

Industrial Demand

World industrial demand for silver, for hundreds of individually small but high-volume uses, is inelastic and price-insensitive at double or even triple 1981 prices. Silver has the whitest color, the best reflectivity, and the best electrical and heat conductivity of any metal. It is second only to gold in its malleability and ductility. One grain of silver (5/100ths of a troy ounce) can be drawn into 400 feet of wire or pounded into leaf 150 times thinner than a piece of paper. Its light sensitivity, for photographic films, is far superior to that of any other known material. One ounce of silver will produce 5,000 color photographs.

The silver-using industries have grown very rapidly since 1940. As they grew larger, they developed many new uses for silver. These two factors have caused the dramatic increase in industrial demand for silver.

Because of its many unique properties, silver has a wide variety of uses in industry. And because of its high value (compared to base metals), it has been and is always used sparingly. Examples of these uses are: photography; plating for electrical contacts, relays and switches; conductor wire for small electronic components and for aircraft spark plugs, corrosion-resistant and highly conductive coating for aluminium bus bars; silver alloy coatings for aircraft engine parts; silver anodes for silver plating; in silver alloys for brazing and soldering; as silver chloride for submarine and torpedo batteries; as part of the amalgam used in silver dental fillings; for compounds used in medicine; coating used in mirrors, photochromic glass and optical and heat-reflecting surfaces. In nearly every case, the amount of silver used represents a very small part of the cost of manufacturing the end product.

Photography

In conventional photography, chemical salts made from silver photochemically react with light in a way that amplifies the impact of each photon of light a billion times and makes it possible to produce photographs of excellent fineness and quality; silver is the only substance known that will do this.

Eastman Kodak, the world's largest film maker, has spent many millions of dollars in research looking for something cheaper than silver that will perform as well. So far, the company has been unsuccessful. Silver is one-hundred times better than the second best light-sensitive substance. The company's conclusion? Nothing else can do the job.[1]

In 1980 alone, there were 26 innovations in *silver halide* systems, including Polaroid's portable instant X-ray film system, which produces 8 × 10 inch X-ray pictures *anywhere*—eliminating the need for a darkroom and allowing for instant analysis of a patient's problem. This system is capable of producing the highest quality images using only one-quarter to one-third the usual X-ray dosage.

A Polaroid executive commenting on his company's 54 major photographic products and 36 different types of film, noted that all of them

> produce images that are available seconds after exposure . . . for applications in medical photography, industrial and scientific recording, in computer graphics and in commercial photography. There is hardly a hospital, laboratory, manufacturing facility or photographic studio that does not use Polaroid instant [silver halide] films, and most of them daily.[2]

Eastman Kodak and Asahi Chemical Industry Company have been successful in using *silver behenate* in improved photographic films which are quickly developed by exposing them to heat after photographic exposure, thereby eliminating the need for wet chemical processing.

Even while calling for greater efforts at recovering silver from photographic scrap, an Eastman Kodak official said that his firm's silver requirements are likely to rise in the years ahead as a result of increased film demand. And the growth in the number of people and industries using "instant" cameras and film of one type or another, from which there is little or no recovery of silver, will reduce the proportion of silver recovered from photographic scrap.

---

[1]"There are no satisfactory alternatives for silver in the photographic processes, and that situation continues to exist despite extensive research in the area of the development of substitute materials which would produce an image comparable to a silver-glazed system."
—National Association of Photographic Manufacturers.

[2]Murray Swindell, Vice President of Sales and Distribution, Polaroid Corporation, September 1980.

The development of electronic photography, still in the early stages of production, will eventually cut into the rise in the use of silver in some segments of photography. This impact, slowing the rate of increase in photographic use of silver, will only begin to be of significance in the second half of this decade. Even this limited impact is probably overstated. In recent decades most innovations of new consumer products which seem to be competitive with existing ones have created new market demands rather than detracting from existing demands. Radio and television, phonograph records and magnetic tape recordings on reels and cassettes, auto cassette hand-held recorders and micro-cassette recorders, 35mm color photography and instant color photography are a few examples of new consumer products co-existing with earlier similar ones while total market demand for old and new increases.

In the United States, the photographic industry uses over 50 million troy ounces of silver a year. Yet, on a cost-per-picture basis, the amount of silver required is negligible (each roll of film contains under 1/100ths of an ounce), representing less than 10 percent of the total cost of a photograph.[3]

When the cost of an essential raw material is so small compared to the cost of the finished product, the demand for the raw material is insensitive to the market price of the raw material. The demand is therefore inelastic.

Electrical and Electronic

In the rapidly expanding electronics industry, three characteristics of silver make it vital for particular applications. It conducts electricity more efficiently than any other metal; it conducts heat more efficiently than any other metal; and it does not oxidize in the air and form an insulating coating as most other metals do.[4]

Wherever silver is used in electronics, only a small amount is required. For instance, most of the tiny diodes used in tran-

[3]Consequently, in any given period the price of silver could double and the price of a roll of film need increase only 10 to 15 percent.

[4]When silver tarnishes, it forms a silver sulfide, not a silver oxide. The importance of this is that metal oxides interfere with the operation of electrical switches, and silver sulfide does not.

sistor circuits contain about 15 cents worth of silver in the connecting wires. The diode itself may cost anywhere from $5 to $50, depending on the type. Silicon solar cells are criss-crossed by silver wire, hearing aids and calculators are powered by silver oxide batteries. The cost of silver for plating switch contacts, of which millions are produced annually, is usually less than 3 percent of the total production cost. Tiny silver discs hardened with tungsten or molybdenum tap together and switch currents from wire to wire in automobiles and light switches. As in photography, the need for silver in the electronics industry represents an extremely price-insensitive, inelastic demand.

Strategic Uses

The U.S. military uses more than 5,000 different items containing silver, ranging from a naval torpedo requiring 4,161 oz. to a particular relay that uses 23 grams. They use over 150 different kinds of bearings containing silver and a wide variety of silver alloys comprised of from 19 to 96 percent silver, according to a Department of Defense release.

Large amounts of silver are used in engines for jet aircraft, rockets, ships, submarines and surface vehicles. Silver is used in spark plugs, distributors, box junctions, switches, relays, magnetos, cable assemblies, points, starters, bearings, clutches, shafts, gears, pistons, sleeves, bushings, linkpins, casings, seals, rings, valves, pumps, actuators, rocket engine nozzles, etc. The U.S. Department of Defense employs over 100 different kinds of batteries containing anywhere from a few grams to thousands of ounces of silver.

The space program employs silver in hundreds of different items, from silver-impregnated ablative nose cones to extreme-temperature resistant, highly conductive tungsten silver rocket engine nozzles, and for a wide variety of electronic and electro-mechanical instruments and devices on the spacecraft and on the ground. Without silver to provide a means of bonding titanium and stainless steel together, the biology experiment instruments on the Mars Viking probe could not have analyzed the plant's surface to make the exciting discovery that the soil there chemically mimics life processes on earth.

Military and space applications demand that all equipment work accurately and reliably. In many vital applications only silver enables equipment to meet these requirements. According to an official report, "The increase in the use of precious metals in both military and civilian commodities has been phenomenal. Indications are that this use will continue or increase in the coming years." Indeed, President Reagan has pledged to build the controversial MX missile, which is reputed to require huge quantities of silver for backup battery systems.

In light of these developments, the decision by Congress to auction the "strategic reserve stockpile" over the next three years seems incomprehensible. In World War II, over about five years, the U.S. government used about 900,000,000 ounces of silver for military purposes — an average of 180,000,000 ounces per year. Yet the strategic reserve stockpile, which had been set aside by the U.S. government for use in event of a new world conflict (World War III), is only 139,500,000 ounces — not enough for even one year based upon comparison with World War II, perhaps much less in view of greatly expanded use of silver in military products since World War II. In the event of a major war, no matter how much per ounce it would be willing to pay, there is no way that the U.S. military could *purchase* the silver it would require for such a conflict. *Confiscation* of all the privately held silver in bar or bulk-coin form in commodity exchange warehouses and bank vaults would yield only enough for the total national need for silver in the first year of World War III! After that . . .?

Other Industrial Uses

In the other industries where silver is used, an inelastic demand also persists. *Silver batteries* have twice the electrical capacity of lead-acid batteries of the same size, and 15 to 20 times the capacity of comparably sized dry cells. This makes silver batteries requisite when size and weight are important considerations. In brazing and soldering, silver's extraordinary malleability, ductility and wetability make it an essential alloying metal. In molten form it adheres easily to other metals and consequently greatly increases a solder or brazing compound's capacity to join metals. The cost of the silver again represents a very small part of the cost of the soldering or brazing job.

For starting automobiles, the heavy lead batteries are quite acceptable. However, for powering portable equipment, rockets, torpedoes, submarines and satellites, etc., the lighter silver batteries are essential. Because of this, the military has been the largest buyer of silver batteries. Demand for various kinds of portably powered civilian appliances in recent years has also grown tremendously.

A new 1-1/2 ounce silver battery developed by Dr. Werner Bohnstedt of West Germany has the capacity to provide temporary emergency power at 1/100 of a second's notice to maintain the power supply to a computer until it can be shut down in a normal manner or connected to some alternate power source.

A 22-pound version of the same kind of silver battery can be used in commercial airliners where hundreds of operations are run by electricity. Within a second the equivalent of 6,700 watts can be generated continuously for three minutes, giving the pilot time to alleviate the electrical problem. The batteries are composed of stacks of paper-thin electrodes containing silver, silver oxide and zinc. They will maintain their readiness for as long as 10 years and are not affected by either high or low temperatures.

In dentistry, medicine and related fields, the cost of the silver used in relation to the cost of the professional service is trivial. In a single silver dime, for instance, there is enough silver for three to four average dental fillings.[5]

Because of the small quantities used individually in most products, the industrial demand for silver is extremely price-inelastic; most uses for silver are so important that they must

---

[5]American mouths cumulatively contain 60 metric tonnes of silver.

be satisfied regardless of the price. In most instances, a doubling or trebling of the price of silver would not increase the price of the end item by more than just a few percent. Thus, the end-product demand for silver is not subject to any significant decrease due to higher prices. The manufacturer-users can and will pay whatever price the market demands for the silver they must have, when they must have it.

Only in the sterlingware industry does the cost of the metal materially affect the demand for the finished articles. In this industry, the cost of silver in the past usually represented 50 to 60 percent of the factory cost of the products, and perhaps 30 to 40 percent of the retail price. With the quadrupling of silver prices in the 1970s (while labor and other production costs about doubled) these percentages have gone up by about 25 percent and very high end-product prices have decreased sales. As can be seen in Table II, page 28, silverware and jewelry is the only category in which silver consumption has declined in the past decade.

Figures so far in 1981 for the U.S. have been registering a substantial increase in eight silver usage categories (contacts, brazing, electroplating, jewelry, photography, dental, catalysts and miscellaneous). In the first quarter of 1981 these eight categories have used a monthly average of 11,265,000 troy ounces compared with a 1980 monthly average of 10,433,000 troy ounces. The U.S. Bureau of Mines puts silver consumption for first-quarter 1981 at 33.8 million ounces, surpassing any quarterly figure for 1980 as a whole. This trend is likely to continue as more and more industrial uses for silver are discovered in today's booming technological atmosphere, evidenced in the following section.

New Developments

In 1980 the Silver Institute reported on 70 new developments of industrial importance which are expanding silver use.[6]

---

[6]*New Silver Technology*, April 1980, (The Silver Institute, 1001 Connecticut Avenue, N.W. Washington, D.C. 20036), one-year subscription, $25.00.

These include improved *silicon-silver cells* for converting sunlight into electric power; new Polaroid *silver halide treated sound tracks: silver-hydrogen batteries;* a *silver-coated mesh* used to convert ozone entering jet airplanes from the upper atmosphere into harmless oxygen; *silver-contining yttrium*, which converts toxic carbon monoxide in the air to carbon dioxide; thin transparent layers of *silver with titanium oxide* for electrically heated windows, which removes frost and ice from automobiles and aircraft.

In the medical field the new uses for silver have continued to grow as quickly as for industry in general. Deep infections can be eliminated by transferring *silver ions* into infected tissues via a very low electric current (this method is used to prevent mastitis, a bacterial infection of cows' udders). *Silver phosphanilate* is a potent antibacterial agent for burn treatments.

These, to name just a few, are some of the recent developments that could only be achieved through the use of silver.

Industries that use silver, a precious metal, do so because they have to. In each case, only silver has characteristics that are vital to the products. In most cases (except sterlingware and jewelry), the amount of silver used in the finished product is quite small. And in all these cases, the cost of metal is insignificant in relation to the price of the finished product. The demand for silver will necessarily continue to increase as these industries grow. Modern industry cannot do without it.

Coinage Demand

While the annual use of silver for official coinage has declined in recent years, official silver coinage is not on the way out.

Table III

Official Silver Coinage, 1970-80
(millions of troy ounces)

Year	Nations Issuing	Ounces Used*	U.S. Gov't Usage
1970	27	27	1
1971	26	27	3
1972	40	38	2.3
1973	56	29	.9
1974	63	28	1.0
1975	67	29	2.7
1976	72	30	1.3
1977	80	23	.4
1978	80	36	.1
1979	99	28	.1
1980	85	16	.1

*(Not including U.S.A.)

Source: The Silver Institute, Handy & Harman.

The very substantial decline in the number of ounces used in 1980 was a direct result of the uncertainty exhibited in the silver market during the year. Many countries that had planned to issue silver coinage in 1980 cancelled or postponed their issues because of the extreme volatility in prices for that year.

What about the future of official precious metal coins? The likelihood is that 1980 was a low point in the striking of silver coins that will not be seen again. There is no way to be sure about this, especially over the next few years. However, there are good reasons to believe that official and/or private use of silver in coins will increase, perhaps dramatically sometime in the 'eighties.

It is even arguable that silver, rather than gold, may be reinstituted as the principal circulating money in the future. At its peak early in 1980 the dollar price of silver was higher than the pre-1971 official $35 gold price (rising 600 percent in 1979), while gold was briefly over $800 per ounce (rising only

200 percent in 1979). If official gold holdings were remonetized as reserves at this level (or higher) as part of a return to an international gold, or gold-exchange standard, global hyperinflation could very well thereby be hastened rather than forestalled. The basis under existing central bank reserve policies would be laid for a twenty-fold increase in national paper-money issues.

Commemorative Coins and Medals

The official use of silver for commemorative coins and medallions has grown substantially in the past decade. In 1980 alone, at least 85 countries issued silver coins in spite of extreme volatility in the silver price. Of those 85 countries, 47 increased coinage from the previous year, including Belgium, the German Democratic Republic, Great Britain, Italy, Mexico, Poland, Sweden, Norway, Venezuela and the U.S.S.R. The People's Republic of China issued its first-ever silver coin in 1980 commemorating the Lake Placid Winter Olympics.

The largest single issue of official coinage was Mexico's "Onza Troy," so named because it contains exactly one troy ounce of .925-fine sterling silver bullion. It was first issued in 1949 when 1,000,000 were minted. Because of increasing demand since the first issue, 4,788,000 were minted in 1978-79 and in 1980 the issue was increased to 5,056,000 coins. In the past, these "Onza Troys" were only available through the Banco de Mexico but today they are bought and sold daily by all Mexican commercial banks, thereby making them a very liquid investment as well as a good store of value. Mexico has not yet promoted these pieces internationally, but apparently has come to recognize silver's role as a store of value and the need for a coin containing one troy ounce of silver.,

The second largest official minting of a silver coin in 1980 came from Italy, with the issuing of 1,500,000 500 lire coins.

The largest and heaviest silver coin currently being issued is in honor of Jamaica's Olympic Gold Medal winners. It is a $25.00 proof 500 fine silver coin measuring 63mm in diameter and weighing 2,100 grains (4.37 ounces).

With the upcoming 1984 Olympic Games, the likelihood is that millions of silver coins will be turned out to commemorate the event. This will add dramatically in 1982 to rising silver consumption figures.

UNICEF is sponsoring a program to be managed by Britain's Royal Mint which will commemorate the International Year of the Disabled Person. These coins will be issued by 24 participating countries and will portray persons of merit or fame who have achieved their positions in spite of disabilities.

In March 1981, a bill was introduced in the U.S. House of Representatives which subsequently passed, authorizing the minting of 10 million, 90 percent silver half-dollars commemorating the 250th anniversary in 1982 of Washington's birth.[7]

Most important however is the burgeoning demand for silver from private mints, for a wide variety of silver coins and medallions of practically every description and for a multitude of purposes — series honoring all the states, all the presidents, various centennials and other anniversary celebrations, commemorating almost uncountable events, people and places.

The world's largest private mint is the Franklin Mint in Philadelphia. There are also private mints in Switzerland, Italy, England and Canada. Franklin Mint may account for over half of the total "collector" coin and medallion business today. In its first full year of operation (1966), Franklin Mint's sales were $1.5 million. In its third year, 1969, sales reached $28 million, of which about half represented silver products. During the 1970s, Franklin diversified into producing a variety of non-precious metal "limited edition collectibles," (porcelain pieces, ornate books, prints, records, etc.) in addition to silver and gold coins. By 1980 total sales had reached $360 million.

Franklin spokesmen do not say how much of those sales are comprised of precious metals items and they jealously (but

---

[7]The list of official government mintings of silver coins for 1980 would be much too long for a complete listing here but is available in a book titled *Modern Silver Coinage — 1980* (The Silver Institute) $10.00.

understandably) refuse to say precisely how much silver or gold Franklin uses. However, the range of the Franklin Mint medals is enormous and their sales campaigns are prodigious.

On the assumption that only 25 percent of 1980 sales were silver items, comprising therefore $90 million at retail, and that 75 percent of that figure was Franklin's cost of silver ($54 million) bought at the 1980 average price of $20.60, then they would have used 2,621,359 ounces. Or, as we are only guessing, let's say around 2½ million ounces. (As Handy and Harman reports a total of 4.2 million ounces of silver was used for such silver coins, medallions and commemorative objects, if our guess is even approximately correct, Franklin alone does account for over half of this business.)

The company sells by mail and is believed to have regular customers buying its medals on a subscription basis, accumulating collections (as do the numismatists and philatelists), and lists half a million prospects who are solicited regularly.

New Private Mints

The prototype of the private mints of the future was founded in 1977 by an imaginative and enterprising young man named Conrad J. Braun. Unlike Franklin Mint's high-priced "collectible" coins, which are sold in limited numbers per issue at 30 to 50 percent more than their metal-content value, Braun's Gold Standard Corporation produces gold and silver coins in high volume and sells them at very low prices. For silver coins there is only a $1 difference between their selling price and their buying price. Gold coins are sold for 5 to 12 percent premium over the daily price of gold, depending on the denomination and quantity ordered.

Mr. Braun's firm is reputed to be the world's largest private gold-minting company. His first one-ounce gold coin, bearing an image of Col. Edward C. Harwood, was launched in 1978 and sales of various sizes and types have since surpassed

500,000 coins (up from 100,000 less than two years ago). So far he has specialized in coins bearing likenesses of prominent free-market economists. Frederick A. Hayek, the 1974 Nobel Laureate adorns the half-ounce coins; Henry Hazlitt, the quarter-ounce; Adam Smith, the tenth-ounce; and Nicholas L. Deak, the twentieth -ounce.

Gold Standard Corporation is located in Kansas City, Missouri and because of the state sales tax, Braun avoids taking orders from Missouri residents. He has plenty of customers in other states, however. On a good day he does about $1,000,000 worth of business; on a slow day, $200,000 — about five times as much as two years ago. With this kind of growth Braun's firm may well become the largest private minter of both gold and silver coins (surpassing Franklin) in 1982. Demand for low-priced silver coins, at very near the spot silver bullion price by weight, is growing at a furious pace for a very good reason — the paper dollar's value is falling like a stone, and growing numbers of people are looking for an alternative.

Braun's gold and silver coins, like the gold Krugerrand and the Mexican silver "Onza Troy"and other low-premium coins being produced by the millions annually and purchased by the public, are coming into increasing use in "barter" exchanges as inflation wears on, and will become more and more used in that way as inflation worsens. Silver coins of low premium and of lower value, more suited to smaller transactions, will be most important.

Braun's approach is sound; if his business is efficient, keeps its costs and charges low and continues to prosper, there is no reason in principle why Braun may not become parent to a global private-enterprise silver and gold standard money. But, of course, he will have a lot of competition. Sunshine Mining Company, for one example, has recently announced plans to mint one-ounce silver medallions to be known as "sunshines."

With the silver price in the $20 to $50 range in most of 1980, two to four times the 1979 range, and four to eight times higher than 1978, it is not surprising that some decline in the use of silver for commemoratives by Franklin and others occurred in the 1978-80 period; they switched to bronze and pewter for some of their "collectibles." However, as noted above, the big growth (from a lower base) is in the low priced, high-value coins produced in volume by Gold Standard Corporation and others, who are rapidly overtaking Franklin. We therefore project that overall private mint usage of silver will climb steeply in the next few years and beyond.

Table IV summarizes the world industrial and coinage demand for silver during the past 21 years.

Table IV

World Silver Consumption, 1960-80
(Excl. Communist countries; millions of troy ounces)

	1960	1961	1962	1963	1964	1965	1966	1967	1968	1969	Total 1960s
Industrial use	225	239	248	261	304	337	355	349	351	366	3,035
Official coinage use (excl. U.S.A.)	58	81	51	56	64	61	76	61	52	36	596
Private coinage use	—	—	—	—	—	—	—	4	7	10	21
Total Consumption	283	320	299	317	368	398	431	414	410	412	3,652

	1970	1971	1972	1973	1974	1975	1976	1977	1978	1979	Total 1970s	1980
Industrial use	339	351	377	446	403	368	399	422	438	420	3,963	440
Official coinage use (excl. U.S.A.)	27	27	38	29	28	29	30	23	36	28	295	16
Private coinage use	11	10	11	22	22	7	9	6	6	5	109	4
Total Consumption	377	388	426	497	453	404	438	451	480	453	4,367	460

Source: Handy & Harman and authors' estimate for 1980.

Investment Demand

To 250 million persons in 51 countries the word for money is the same as the word for silver, and silver literally means money. When French-speaking people in Europe, Africa, Asia and the Americas speak of silver, they call it "argent," if they are talking about money the word also is "argent." Similarly, Spanish-speaking people the world-over use the word "plata" to mean silver, money or both.

In both languages where something other than the literal words for silver or gold are used as the word for money, the word usually is the name of the unit of weight in which silver or gold was measured or is the name of the first widely used silver or gold coin.

> The Biblical "talent" of the New Testament (*talanton* in Greek) is both a coin and a measure. The corresponding Hebrew word of the Old Testament (*kikkar*) is a (silver) coin. . . Other Biblical coins are the "shekel," sometimes slangily used today, and the "mite" (about one-quarter of a cent but with a vastly greater purchasing power in those days).
>
> The (silver) *drachma* and *mna* were among the popular coins of ancient Greece; the former survives in the druggist's "dram." The Romans had the *nummus*, from which we get "numismatics," the lore of coins, . . . The "pistole" was a gold coin of France and Spain; . . . A *grivna* was an ancient Russian silver coin, the equivalent of one pound of silver. . .
>
> The "dollar" got its name from the German *Thaler*, short for Joachimsthaler, coined from silver mined in Joachimsthal, Bohemia, in . . . (the 16th century) . . . when English pounds, shillings, and pence, French *livres tournois*, *Louis d'or*, and pistoles, Portuguese Johannes, or "joes," Dutch ducats, guilders, and florins, and even Swedish rix dollars were current. . .
>
> Spanish has two words for "dollar," beside the borrowed *dolar*. They are *peso* and *duro*. One refers to the weight of a silver dollar, since the original meaning of *peso* is "weight," the other to its consistency (*duro* means "hard," somewhat like the Latin *solidus* at an earlier date) . . . Both the *rupee* of India and the *rupiyah* of Indonesia come from a root meaning "silver". . .
>
> Among the currencies of modern states. . .both *lira* and the pound sterling were originally one pound of silver.[8]

With approximately half of the world's marketable gold in official vaults and with only about one-tenth of the available

---

[8]Excerpted from *The Story of Language*, Mario Pei, (J. B. Lippincott Co., Philadelphia & New York, 1965) pp. 236, 237, 238.

silver coin and bullion there (nine-tenths being in private ownership), the world would be far better off and would escape inflation entirely in the future if private markets were to reinstitute silver coins, and fully redeemable silver certificates as circulating money. Were this done ahead of the final hyperinflation of national currencies, then all of that surplus official paper could readily be exchanged for the new silver money as an uninflatable replacement. And the world could escape the economic chaos of a total absence of a medium of exchange that could otherwise occur in the aftermath of the coming global hyperinflation.

Throughout the ages, again and again, governments have tried to short-change the public with base-metal coins and unbacked paper money; in short they have tried hundreds of times to operate an exclusive monopoly of counterfeiting! It has always failed, sooner or later.

What finally makes unbacked paper money and base-metal coins go out of style, of course, is officialdom itself; they get too greedy, print too much, and in time you need a bushel basket of paper money to buy a pair of shoes; just a little later the bushel basket will not be enough for a loaf of bread. By then nobody will even take the paper money (preferring cigarettes or chocolate bars instead), and the money system breaks down completely. There is no way even to guess how soon this will happen again in America (as it did in Colonial days), but we are on that track. It could develop in only a few years with just a little more momentum than we have now. In any case, we expect it to happen in three to seven years, if recent trends continue.[9]

Apart from an uncertain time-scale, it *is* certain that we are headed in that direction and will be, as far into the future as present trends give anyone a clue for predicting. For this reason, at least for the next few years, the demand for precious metals as a safe refuge for scared capital is going to increase, and increase, and increase.

---

[9]See *The Coming Currency Collapse — And What You Can Do About It* (1980: Books in Focus, New York) for a discussion of these economic trends.

CHAPTER IV

Silver Supplies

We now turn to the other side of the silver equation: supply. Each year, silver demand is satisfied from three sources: mine and secondary production, and existing aboveground stocks. Because there is a sizable gap between the total demand for silver and the amounts produced, these aboveground stocks are dwindling year by year and in terms of the 1960s have virtually disappeared.

Mine Production

Most of the earth's silver is found in the Western Hemisphere—primarily Mexico, the United States, Peru and Canada, and following those countries, a few other South and Central American countries. There is no large silver production in Africa, Asia or Europe. The only free-world country that produces any substantial amount of silver outside the Western Hemisphere is Australia. Even though gold is produced in great quantities in South Africa, and silver is often a by-product of gold production, little silver is produced there because silver just isn't found at the great depths from which 90 percent of South Africa's gold is mined.

The production of silver and gold (and in fact all other metals) has increased over the last century, and, excepting silver, especially in the last half-century. A close look at Chart 4 reveals an important difference in the long term trend of mine production for silver and gold. In the last half-century the production of silver has leveled off at a definite plateau.

Chart 4
World Production—Gold Vs. Silver

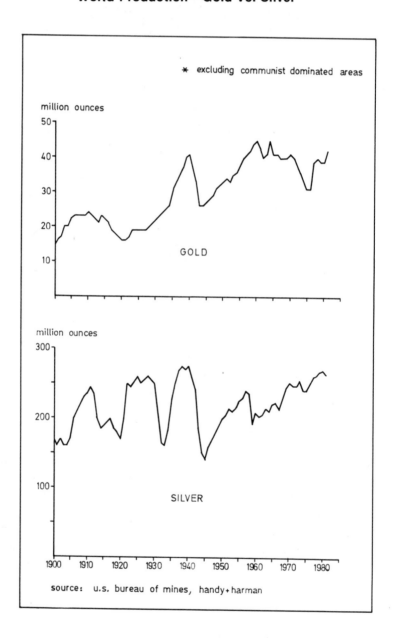

The lower part of Chart 4 shows silver production leveling out around 250 million troy ounces. The production of gold continued to rise steadily until the beginning of the 1970s when higher prices made it profitable in South Africa to process lower-grade ores, causing production to decline from its earlier peaks. The subsequent decline in gold prices in the mid-1970s necessitated a return to the processing of high-grade ores, thus increasing the level of mine production to recent levels.

There are two major reasons for the different configuration of these production trends. The first one is the geological factor—the unusual way in which silver is deposited in the earth. In many parts of the world, for instance in Mexico, the United States, the Soviet Union, Peru, Australia and Canada, silver has occasionally occurred in nature as pure metal, uncombined with any other substance. It has occurred most often, however, and in highest concentration at or near the surface of the earth. Geologists call this characteristic "epithermal deposition." They explain that eons ago, when the molten earth was cooling, silver condensed near the surface. As a result, throughout history the richest deposits of silver, such as those in the formerly rich Comstock Lode in western Nevada, have been found right at the surface of the earth. In older and deeper mines, less silver is found per ton of ore mined, until it finally peters out. Older, deeper mines produce less silver, and at a higher cost. All over the earth (wherever silver has been found), the richest and most easily found deposits have occurred at the upper levels. The deeper the excavation necessary to get to the deposits, the poorer the deposits.[1] The difficulty in locating new deposits is much greater, and the likelihood of finding rich ones is much less today than in times past.

The second major factor limiting silver production is an economic factor: the production of silver depends to a large extent on the demand for and the annual production of copper, lead and zinc. About 75 percent of the world's silver comes not from silver mines as such, but as a by-product or co-product of these other three metals.

Chart 5 shows the production of silver since 1900 compared with the production of copper, lead and zinc. The annual pro-

---

[1]An apparent exception is in the Coeur d'Alene area in Idaho; however, the deposits now found at about the 5,000-foot level appear to have originally been surface deposits.

Chart 5
World Production of Copper, Lead and Zinc Vs. Silver*

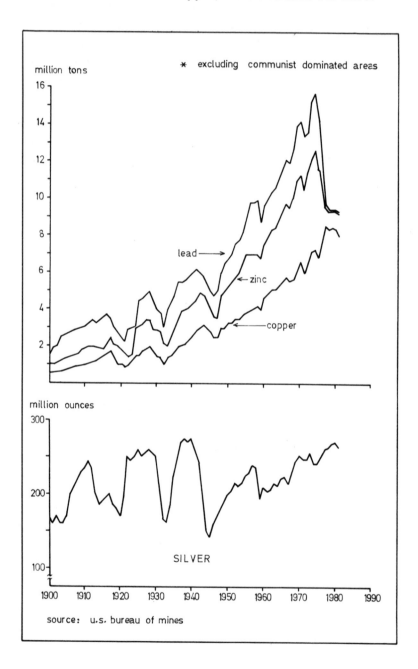

million tons

＊ excluding communist dominated areas

lead——→

←zinc

←—copper

million ounces

SILVER

source: u.s. bureau of mines

duction of the three base metals has increased substantially over this period. The increase could be expected because of: (1) the general expansion of industrial production over this period, and (2) the mechanization and modernization of the mining industry over the same period. But the production of silver has not increased as rapidly as the other metals. What factors have held it down?

A major part of the answer, again, is the geological factor, epithermal deposition. Whether silver is obtained from a rich silver lode or as a by-product in the production of base metals, the deeper the mine, the less silver in the ore. Most other metals, including copper, lead and zinc, are deposited in veins of roughly equal richness at all levels. When the veins turn downward into the earth, the ore may contain the same amount or even more base metal but there will be less and less silver. Consequently, because of the geologic and economic factors, the production of silver has not kept pace with the production of other metals in recent decades.

Furthermore, a large percentage of the annual production of copper, lead, and zinc is obtained by melting down scrap metal. About 40 percent of the lead, 30 percent of the zinc and 15 percent of the copper smelted is recovered from scrap metal. Obviously, "production" from scrap metal produces no by-product silver.

Silver is an extreme example of what economists call "inelastic supply," a situation in which the amount produced is insensitive to the market price. With most things, if the price goes up, production will increase; if the price goes down, production will decrease. However, a product such as silver — mostly a by-product of the production of other metals — does not respond to the market price in this way; so the supply is called "inelastic."

To illustrate: Suppose you are operating a lead and zinc mine, with 80 percent of your annual sales revenue coming from lead and zinc and 20 percent from silver. Now assume that the prices of lead and zinc double. You naturally increase your production.

But make a different assumption. Assume that the price of lead and/or zinc falls substantially and the price of silver doubles. To increase the production of silver you must also increase the production of lead and zinc. You could well end up with so much lead and zinc you would not be able to market them except at a loss. Do you speed up your operation to respond to the higher silver prices? Only if the market can absorb the increased production of lead and zinc at a profitable price. If many producers do this, it will obviously become impossible to market the higher total production profitably.

This is precisely what has happened since nonferrous metals production peaked in 1974 (see Chart 5); for one example,

> . . .Kellogg, the Silver Valley's largest community, with some 4,000 residents, is mainly a one-company town, and the company, Bunker Hill Co., a subsidiary of Gulf Resources & Chemical Corp., is closing after nearly 100 years of operation. To be shut by year's end are its two underground mines, which produce lead, zinc and silver, and its zinc plant and lead smelter. The operations sustained a pretax loss of $7.7 million in the first half of this year, and company officials say they don't see any improvement in the second half.
>
> . . .The damage at Bunker Hill has resulted mostly from a sharp fall in the demand for lead and zinc used in autos. . .
>
> Still another dimension is that the Bunker Hill Complex produces about 15% of the nation's silver and 20% of its lead and zinc. Mining experts say that the loss of the facilities will be a blow to the nation's mining industry. . .[2]

As can be seen in the top half of Chart 5, lead and zinc production plunged dramatically in the 1974 recession and have still not recovered their previous peaks. Copper production, on the other hand, rose during the 1974-78 period, creating a copper glut on the markets since 1978 which resulted in lower prices for the metal. Consequently, since 1977, the trend in copper production has been down while lead and zinc production have leveled out in the same period.

So the level of production of silver depends not so much on its market price, but primarily on the market for the associated base metals, copper, lead and zinc. Both the production and the consumption of these metals, which are principally consumed by the electrical and automotive industries, are highly sensitive to business conditions. Demand for these metals, and their rate of production—and therefore the production of by-product silver—drops more sharply than silver consumption activity in a recession or depression.

---

[2] The *Wall Street Journal*, September 8, 1981.

Thus, silver tends to become relatively more scarce and more valuable in a prolonged recession or depression as well as in a period of expanding business activity. This fact and the price-insensitivity of production levels to soaring prices are evident in Chart 6.

Two important things, then, affect the mine supply of silver. The first is the geological consideration — older, deeper mines produce less silver. The second is the economic consideration — because most silver production is by-product production, the market price of silver does not appreciably affect overall production. The analysis of these two considerations indicates that the production of silver will remain quite inflexible and possibly even decrease in the future.[3]

Chart 7 shows the deficit between industrial consumption alone and mine production for the past two decades.

High and increasing wage and other costs, more than demand bidding, have pushed prices up in the copper, lead and zinc markets, despite adequate supplies and production. This has caused the biggest users of these metals to cut consumption whenever possible — reducing demand. It has caused stepped-up scrap recovery efforts in the lead-acid battery business, and substitution of plastics for zinc in many automobile parts and other die castings. It has caused the major "long lines" electric utilities to switch to aluminum high-voltage transmission cables.

Conversely, it is characteristic of the "by-product" silver market that increasing store-of-value monetary (hard money) demand pulled prices up in the 1970s. In 1983 and beyond, increasingly insistent *user* demand *and* intensified hard-money demand can be expected to pull prices up far beyond the prior peak levels.

---

[3]President Johnson, in his letter to Congress of June 3, 1965 declared in support of the coinage act of 1965 (which eliminated silver from U.S. coinage):

"There is no dependable or likely prospect that new, economically workable sources of silver may be found that could appreciably narrow the gap between silver supply and demand. The optimistic outlook is for an increase in production of about 20 percent over the next four years. This would be of little help. Further, because silver is produced chiefly as a by-product of the mining of copper, lead and zinc, even a very large increase in the price of silver would not stimulate silver production sufficiently to change the outlook." (In fact, the actual four-year increase in production from 1965 to 1969 was only 12 percent, from 218 to 245 million troy ounces, in spite of a 1966-68 price increase of 62 percent.)

Chart 6
Silver Production Vs. Price

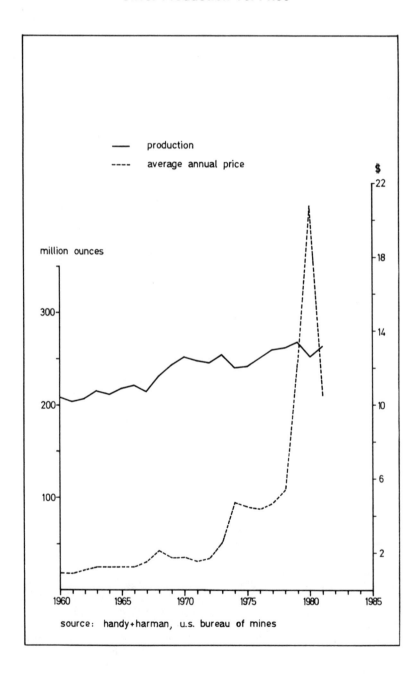

Chart 7
Silver Deficit 1960-1981

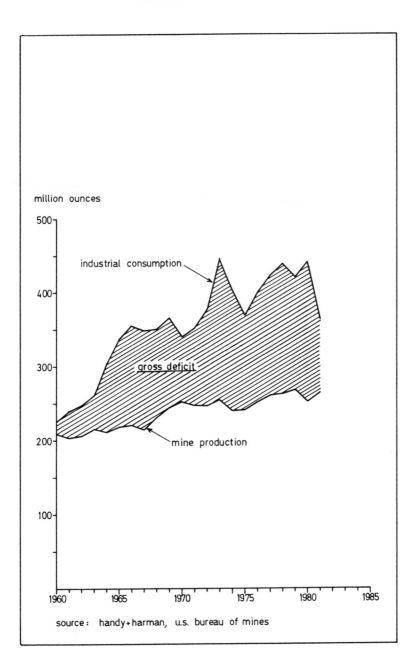

million ounces

industrial consumption

gross deficit

mine production

source: handy+harman, u.s. bureau of mines

Secondary Production

Only limited data is available on the total amount of scrap silver recovered in industrial manufacturing, because the scrap recovery programs of most large silver users are "in plant." However, for our purposes, this particular lack of precise data does not matter because the figures that are collected and reported for annual industrial *use* are actually amounts purchased in the report year, and are therefore the *net* amount that is actually consumed, by each reporting company and therefore by industry as a whole.

The figures that are reported for secondary production are salvage sales amounts, which represent scrap that cannot be recovered directly by the plant generating the scrap, but which is collected and sold as scrap and finds its way back to a refinery to be processed. In the decades preceding the 1960s, only about 8 percent of the annual production of silver was from scrap recovery. Substantial price increases for silver in the 1970s stimulated stepped-up recovery efforts, particularly by the U.S. government and within the photographic industry; silver scrap recovery has been increased in recent years to about 25 percent of total production. However, with recovery techniques now optimized, this percentage is not likely to increase in the future; it may even decline as readily obtainable scrap supplies become depleted. Salvage sales reported also include private coin-melting, which occurred in sizable amounts in the late 1960s and in massive amounts throughout the 1970s.

In the 1960s worldwide salvage sales including private coin-melting, on average yielded only about 26 million ounces yearly. In the 1970s much higher prices trebled the salvage of silver from all sources, from 30 million ounces to about 90 million ounces. with an average annual rate of 67 million ounces over the decade. Salvage sales, spurred by extremely high prices, probably peaked in 1980.

Table V summarizes the supply of silver from mine and secondary production, for the past 21 years.

Table V

World Silver Production, 1960-80
(Excl. Communist countries; millions of troy ounces)

	1960	1961	1962	1963	1964	1965	1966	1967	1968	1969	Total 1960s
Mine Production	208	203	206	215	211	218	221	214	231	244	*2,171*
Secondary production (salvage sales, private coin melt)	21	29	7	11	36	7	59	53	84	27	*334*
Total Production	229	232	213	226	247	225	280	267	315	271	*2,505*

	1970	1971	1972	1973	1974	1975	1976	1977	1978	1979	Total 1970s	1980
Mine Production	252	247	246	254	240	241	251	260	262	268	*2,521*	270
Secondary production (salvage sales, private coin melt)	30	35	45	60	66	73	86	94	96	81	*666*	121
Total Production	282	282	291	314	306	314	337	354	358	349	*3,187*	391

Source: Handy & Harman.

Aboveground Stocks

When the world's annual silver consumption for industry and coinage are added together, the comparison with annual production is dramatic. Each year in the past two decades (see Table VI), the world has for all purposes used on average over 100 million ounces more silver than has been produced. Chart 8 shows the staggering deficit between production and consumption in the past twenty-one years.

Since 1957, total silver consumption has exceeded total pro-

Table VI
World Silver Deficit, 1960-1980
(Excl. Communist countries; millions of troy ounces)

	1960	1961	1962	1963	1964	1965	1966	1967	1968	1969	Total 1960s	1970	1971	1972	1973	1974	1975	1976	1977	1978	1979	Total 1970s	1980
Industrial use	225	239	248	261	304	337	355	349	351	366	3,035	339	351	377	446	403	368	399	422	438	420	3,963	440
Official coinage use (excl. U.S.A.)	58	81	51	56	64	61	76	61	52	36	596	27	27	38	29	28	29	30	23	36	28	295	16
Private coinage use	—	—	—	—	—	—	—	4	7	10	21	11	10	11	22	22	7	9	6	6	5	109	4
Mine production	208	203	206	215	211	218	221	214	231	244	2,171	252	247	246	254	240	241	251	260	262	268	2,521	270
Secondary production (salvage sales, private coin melt)	21	29	7	11	36	7	59	53	84	27	334	30	35	45	60	66	73	86	94	96	81	666	121
Total production	229	232	213	226	247	225	280	267	315	271	2,505	282	282	291	314	306	314	337	354	358	349	3,187	391
Surplus (deficit)	(54)	(88)	(86)	(91)	(121)	(173)	(151)	(147)	(95)	(141)	(1147)	(95)	(106)	(135)	(183)	(147)	(90)	(101)	(97)	(122)	(104)	(1180)	(69)

Average yrly. deficit for 1960s: 114.7 mil. troy ozs.

Average yrly. deficit for 1970s: 118 mil. troy ozs.

Source: Handy and Harman and authors' estimate for 1980.

Chart 8
Total Silver Demand Vs. Total Production

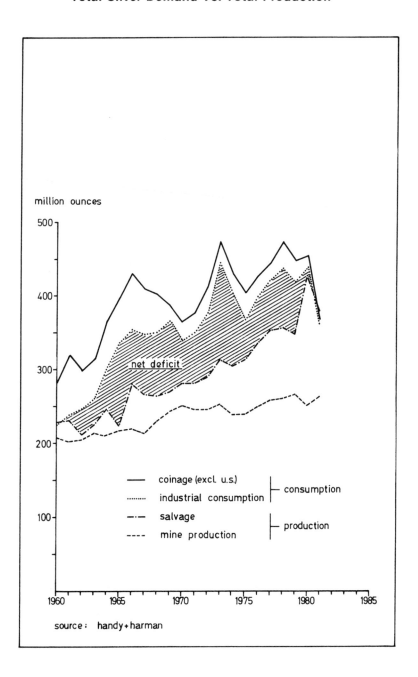

million ounces

net deficit

—— coinage (excl. u.s.)	⎱ consumption
.... industrial consumption	⎰
—·— salvage	⎱ production
---- mine production	⎰

source : handy + harman

duction in every year except 1980 (when the price zoomed to a record $50 per ounce). Where has all the silver come from during the past 23 years to fill the huge gap between production and consumption? The most sizable stock in existence during that period was held by the U.S. Treasury.

U.S. Treasury Stocks

Chart 9 shows how the United States supplemented world silver production by flooding the market with silver from its reserves. In 1958, the U.S. Treasury had 2.1 billion troy ounces of silver in its vaults. This is a lot of silver; in fact, it is 10 percent of all the silver that had been mined in the world since 1500. It took 465 years to produce 22 billion troy ounces of silver; it took about 90 years for the United States to accumulate 2.1 billion troy ounces;[4] but it took only 12 years, from 1958 to 1970, for the U.S. to dissipate these reserves virtually entirely.[5]

In 1967, after losing three-quarters of its stock, the Treasury stopped sales at the $1.29 price and restricted sales at "auction prices" to legitimate domestic industrial users only. This ended 34 years of direct price control in silver. The silver price moved abruptly to $1.70, and on up to a 1968 high of $2.56. In mid-1968, when silver-certificate redemptions were halted, the U.S. Treasury (in a surprise move) began dumping its hoard of coin-melt silver into the market, stretching the General Services Administration (GSA) weekly sales, and depressing silver prices through 1972.

Foreign Government and Smuggled Supplies

There are no longer any sizable hoards of silver in the world; nor can there ever again be any as large as the hoard that was held in the U.S. Treasury in 1960. Foreign govern-

---

[4]This accumulation began in 1878 with passage of the Bland-Allison Silver Purchase Act (see Chapter I).

[5]The U.S. Treasury ran out of silver to sell on November 10, 1970, retaining only 22 million ounces, which along with 25 million ounces obtained from the "strategic" reserves were used for minting the "Ike" part-silver dollar.

Chart 9
U.S. Gov't Silver Stocks as of Dec. 31, 1960-1981

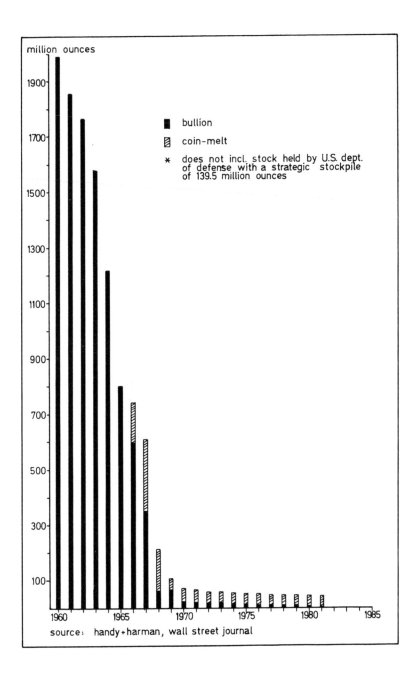

ment stocks totaled less than 10 percent of the U.S. holdings at that time.

Nevertheless, recovery by foreign governments of silver from demonetized coin added substantially to world supplies in the '70s, at an average per-year rate of 30 million ounces; silver bullion sales of foreign governments averaged 14 million ounces. These two sources together averaged 44 million ounces per year in the decade but were a lesser and diminishing part of the total supply late in the 1970s as the remaining supply of foreign coins to be melted steadily declined.

A further source of supply during the '70s came from the Far East. The citizens of Asian countries, notably India and Pakistan, hold large amounts of silver, but it is mostly in the form of art objects and ornaments owned by individuals in small amounts and dispersed throughout Asia. However, smuggled silver from these sources averaged about 44 million ounces per year during the decade.

Private Stockpiles

Over the decades, until 1970, large amounts of silver sold by the Treasury moved into private inventories. These inventories, at an all-time peak level in 1970 (see Chart 10), were sufficient, along with secondary supply flows, to meet the supply/demand gap through the 1970s. Some liquidation of such holdings in investment and speculative hands began in 1971 and continued each year until 1980 as the silver price rose and the trend of these private reserve stocks continued downward. Speculative stocks rose from 141 million ounces in 1979 to 164 million ounces in 1980. New York Commodity Exchange Warehouse stocks in the first quarter of 1981 dropped 1.296 million ounces; at the Chicago Board of Trade for the same period, stocks dropped by 15.198 million ounces, the biggest drop since silver trading began (see Chart 11).

The silver stocks held in commodity exchange depositories in New York and Chicago, which are deliverable against futures contracts, are by far the largest visible supplies of silver presently available to offset somewhat the growing silver deficit. However, the often overlooked fact is that these stocks are not owned by the commodity exchanges. They are

Chart 10
Remaining Aboveground Stocks of Silver

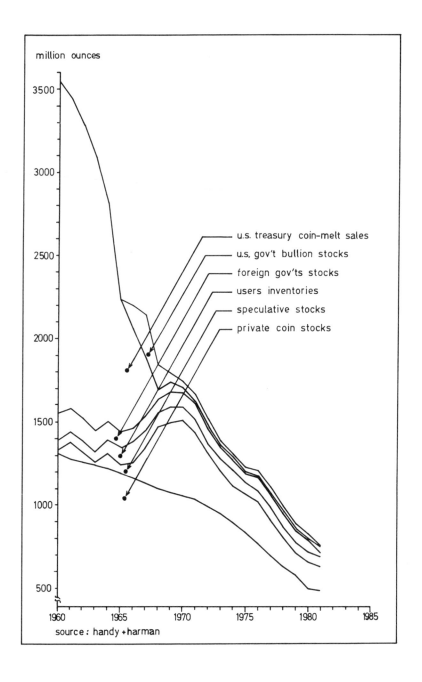

million ounces

- u.s. treasury coin-melt sales
- u.s. gov't bullion stocks
- foreign gov'ts stocks
- users inventories
- speculative stocks
- private coin stocks

source : handy + harman

Chart 11
Commodity Exchange Warehouse Silver Stocks Versus
Silver Price

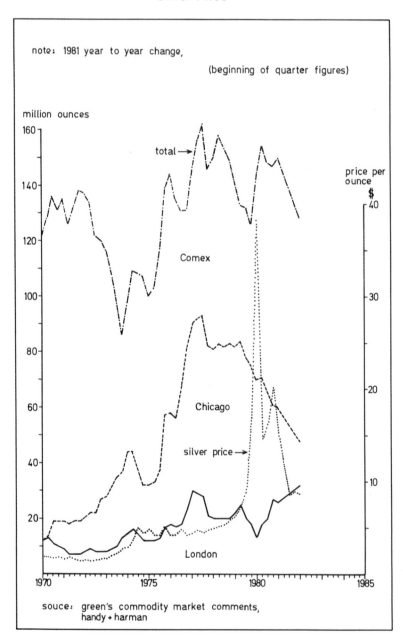

note: 1981 year to year change,

(beginning of quarter figures)

million ounces

souce: green's commodity market comments,
         handy + harman

the property of silver traders and private investors who have taken delivery of future contracts for purposes of their own. The price at which these holders are willing to sell will have a great deal to do with when or whether these stocks become available to industrial users.

There was a 6 percent decline in warehouse inventories during 1978, to 141.1 million ounces. During 1979 these inventories were depleted further. As Chart 11 shows, total stocks at the three exchanges had been falling until 1980, after an extended rise from mid-1973 to late 1977. In 1980, following the spectacular rise of silver to almost $50 per ounce and the correspondingly dramatic decline to the 1981 low of $8, investors rebuilt the warehouse stocks to pre-1978 levels at 148.1 million ounces for 1980 yearend (Table VII). Chart 11 also shows the price of silver over the same period. It is clear that there is a significant inverse correlation between the size of the warehouse stocks and the price. That is, as stocks generally go up the price generally comes down, and when the stocks generally come down the price generally rises.

There appears no doubt that investor's and user's attention will be increasingly focused on the Commodity Exchange Silver stocks, and that silver prices will become increasingly sensitive to their level changes — the price advancing on the decline of the stocks and declining on any stock increases. And, as the production/consumption figures show, the declining trend for warehouse stocks should continue.

Chart 12 depicts speculative and user inventories based on the assumption that both were at a minimum level in 1960 and adding to the total (top line) all speculative purchases since 1960, less speculative sales. The magnitude and movement of user inventory levels is calculated on the basis of a normal level in 1960 of a three-month supply. Based upon industrial purchasing practice, this is a high estimate for such an expensive, readily available raw material. The movement of this line slightly above or below the currently applicable three-month supply level partially "smooths-out" the irregular year-to-year deviations in reported industrial use (which in reality is reported industrial purchases) and the long-term trend of industrial use. Movement of the user inventory line

Table VII

Silver Bullion Inventories Available
(excluding U.S. Treasury stocks and U.S. strategic
reserve — millions of troy ounces at yearend)

	1980	1981
Exchange-Approved Warehouse Inventories		
New York Commodity Exchange	86.6	77.6
Chicago Board of Trade	34.2	15.5
London Metal Exchange	27.3	32.2
Total	148.1	125.3
Other Inventories		
U.S. industry stocks		
(as of December 31)		
U.S. Defense Department stocks	30.0	19.8*
(as of December 31)	4.0	3.8*
Stocks of foreign governments (est).	72.0	72.0
Unreported stocks in U.S. and abroad		
(est.)	75.0	100.0
Total	181.0	195.6
Total Inventories	329.1	320.0
Increase (decrease) in inventories		(9.1%)

Source: Handy & Harman.

does not affect the top line (total). When it exceeds three months' supply the above-normal amount, in effect, it is speculative held inventory in user stocks.

Where is this speculatively held silver? More than one-fourth of it is in the Commodity Exchange Warehouse in New York (85.352 million ounces, at last report), another 27 million ounces or so is in London bank vaults, 60 million ounces are in silver users' and refiners' in-plant inventories and the remainder is in Exchange vaults in Chicago, Zurich,

Chart 12
Privately-Held Silver

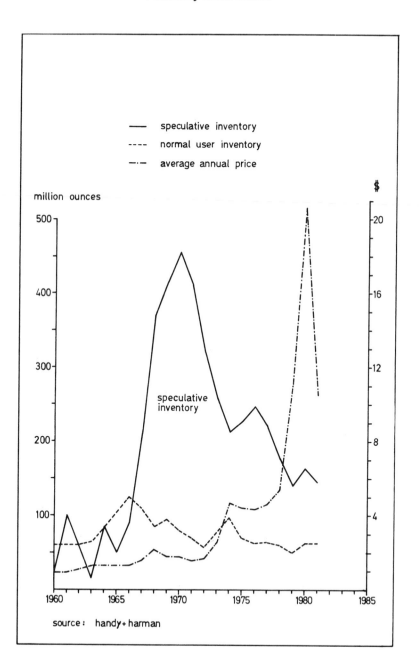

legend:
— speculative inventory
---- normal user inventory
—·— average annual price

million ounces

speculative
inventory

source: handy+harman

Frankfurt and Paris. There are also many scattered small amounts in other locations around the world.

Most of the market-warehouse, investor-owned and speculatively held silver is owned by individuals and companies who expect silver to command higher prices in the future. Probably much of it is owned by industrial silver users themselves who plan to take delivery in increments in the coming years to supplement deliveries they will be receiving under long-term contracts with metals mining and refining companies. This user-owned silver is, in effect, industrial inventory just as though it were physically stored in these various companies' warehouses. It is not for sale. It is held for use. When these user-owned stocks are withdrawn and used in the next year or two, these companies will have to purchase some silver from those who own the other half (approximately) of the exchange warehouse stocks, the individual investors and speculators.

CHAPTER V

Total Silver Supplies and Demands Compared and Projected

The erratic course of the price of silver since 1967 is due, at bottom, to three things:

(1) Government market manipulation.
(2) Misinformation by government and by private sources, including the producer interests (overly bright reports) and user interests (overly dismal reports).
(3) Commodity-exchange rule manipulation by exchange officials.

Every year, for many years, bills have been proposed in the Congress with urges from the Silver Users Association to sell the U.S. government strategic stockpile (139.5 million ounces in 1981) of silver. Finally, in 1981, Congress announced that 105 million ounces of this silver will be auctioned off over the next three years. However, at the last auction for 1981, all bids for that silver were rejected by the General Services Administration. Altogether only 2 million ounces were sold since Congress passed the auction bill.

The GSA weekly auction has subsequently been suspended and they have been required to conduct a study of the silver disposal program to be submitted to congress on July 1, 1982. The following quotation on the bill appeared in Green's Commodity Market Comments, Vol., XVII, No. 1, 1/13/82: "In it GSA will have to justify the sales as well as the method of disposal of silver from the national stockpile. It is our belief that no silver auction in the form of bullion will be reinstated.

Table VIII
World Silver Demand, Supply, Stocks—1960 through 1981
(millions of ounces)

	1960	1961	1962	1963	1964	1965	1966	1967	1968	1969	Total 1960s	1970	1971	1972	1973	1974	1975	1976	1977	1978	1979	Total 1970s	1980	1981
Annual Demand																								
Industrial Use	225	239	248	261	304	337	355	349	351	366	3035	339	351	377	446	403	368	399	422	438	420	3063	440	363
Official Coinage Use (Except U.S.; see note)	58	81	51	56	64	61	76	61	52	36	596	27	27	38	29	28	29	30	23	36	28	295	14	6
Private Coinage Use	0	0	0	0	0	0	0	4	7	10	21	11	10	11	22	22	7	9	6	6	5	109	5	4
New Speculative Buys	0	75	0	0	70	0	40	120	160	45	510	40	0	0	0	0	16	20	0	0	0	76	26 †	49
Total Annual Mkt. Demand	283	395	299	317	438	398	471	534	570	457	4162	417	388	426	497	453	420	458	451	480	453	4443	485	422
Annual Supply																								
Mine Production	208	203	206	215	211	218	221	214	231	244	2171	252	247	246	254	240	241	251	260	262	268	2521	253	264
Salvage Sales (Incl. Private Coin-Melt)	21	29	7	11	36	7	59	53	34	27	947	30	35	45	60	66	73	86	94	96	81	666	176	117
U.S. Treas. Mkt. Sales	21	63	1	25	151	80	142	195	180	89	249	68	2	2	1	1	3	1	0	0	0	78	0	2
Foreign Gov't. Sales: Bullion	22	71	30	10	20	26	20	13	15	22	288	10	15	10	42	11	15	7	5	8	10	133	5	2
Demonetized Coin-Melt	10	30	20	15	20	30	28	35	50	50	284	25	25	15	39	47	35	43	25	23	25	302	55	12
Exports From Far East	0	0	0	0	0	0	0	22	60	25	107	32	19	19	39	42	53	70	41	45	34	394	45	34
New Speculative Sales	0	0	35	40	0	35	0	0	0	0	110	0	45	90	62	46	0	0	26	46	35	350	0	0
Total Annual Mkt. Supply	282	299	299	316	438	396	470	532	570	457	4156	417	388	427	497	453	420	458	451	480	453	4444	534	431

Aboveground Stocks																							
U.S. Gov't. Stocks (Bullion) (see note below*)	1992	1862	1767	1582	1214	796	592	348	59	61	10273	18	16	14	13	12	9	7	6	6	6	4	2
U.S. Treasury Coin-Melt Sales	0	0	0	0	0	0	150	260	150	51	611	48	45	41	42	41	40	40	39	39	39	39	39
Foreign Gov't Stocks**	158	142	137	127	107	90	80	85	80	90	1096	85	95	90	60	60	50	82	77	79	75	20	8
Users' "Regular" Inventory	60	60	60	65	85	105	125	110	85	95	850	80	70	58	77	98	69	62	66	60	50	60	60
Speculatively Held Stocks	25	100	65	15	85	50	90	210	370	415	1425	455	410	320	258	212	228	248	222	176	141	167	145
Private Coin Stocks***	1310	1280	1260	1245	1225	1195	1167	1132	1102	1080	11996	1055	1030	990	945	895	835	770	695	630	580	490	483
Total Remaining Aboveground Stocks in all forms**	3545	3444	3289	3034	2716	2236	2204	2145	1846	1792	26251	1741	1666	1513	1395	1318	1231	1269	1105	990	891	780	737
Note: U.S. Coinage Use from U.S. Treasury Stocks	46	56	77	112	203	320	54	44	37	19	968	1	2	1	1	1	3	1	0	0	0	0	0

* U.S. Gov't. Strategic Reserve Stock of 139.5 mil. oz. not included.

** Does not include Red China, who in 1960 had a stock estimated at 100 mil. oz. from which 90 mil. oz. were sold in 1960, '61, and '62 (included in Foreign Gov't. Bullion Sales above). Also excludes India, from which private silver bullion export is legally barred. (Some smuggling of coin-melt and utensil-jewelry salvage silver nevertheless occurs each year and is included in the supply table above.) Russian silver stocks, not known but believed quite small, also are not included. Communist-bloc silver sales to the West in recent years have ranged from zero to a maximum of 11 mil. oz. in any one year. With the expansion of silver-using industries in Russia, is expected to become a buyer of silver in western markets in the future.

*** The total amount of non-numismatic coins remaining that could be expected to be melted eventually.

**** Excluding silverware, jewelry, medallions and other fabricated forms which are not normally more than an incidental factor in salvage (re-cycling) supply and Far Eastern exports which are included in *Annual Supply* above.

† Handy and Harman's 1981 report revised their 1980 report on 1980 industrial consumption to 350 mil. oz. and net spec buys to 116 mil. oz. we retain their 1980 figures as more realistic; total consumption is the same.

What alternate methods of disposal will eventually evolve is difficult to predict, but we expect that the General Accounting Office report on the subject .of silver sales, which was requested by Congress independently from the one requested from GSA, will make a sufficiently strong case against silver bullion auctions to free the market from this worry once and forever."

Commercial misinformation has also often affected both sides of the market. On the producer side, there has been a failure to consider the full impact of the various governments' bullion and coin-melt sales in both the '60s and the '70s; and on the user side there has been failure to consider the coming impact of the worldwide absence of any flow of government and/or coin-melt silver into the markets in the mid-1980s. We can now put these matters into perspective. The effects of the U.S. Treasury's much-extended silver sales program in the late '60s and early '70s had been: (1) above-normal private inventories, and (2) below-normal market prices throughout the 1970s (compared to what prices would otherwise have been). However, the immutable law of supply and demand has not been repealed, and with the prospect that the U.S. government and other governments will soon be completely out of the silver market for the first time (and unable to re-enter it *except as buyers*) it is now possible *for the first time* to collect, organize, analyze and project virtually pure market data.

Review of the 1960s

In the decade of the 1960s, the U.S. Treasury had supplied a total of 947 million ounces of silver to world markets through its bullion sales (over half of this came from melted pre-1965 silver coins it withdrew from circulation in the late '60s). It also churned out 986 million ounces of silver coins in the first half of the decade — melting about half of these in the second half of that decade (in both cases more than all other nations combined).

The production/consumption deficit for the decade totalled about 1.08 billion ounces. It was met as follows: .54 billion ounces from U.S. Treasury stock and melted U.S. coinage and .53 billion ounces from sales of bullion and demonetized coin-melt by foreign governments whose stocks were thus relatively depleted by the beginning of the '70s and fell to an insignificant level at the beginning of the '80s. U.S. Treasury stocks, which changed little in the 1950s, were completely depleted for all practical purposes in the late '60s and early '70s.

Review of the 1970s

In the decade of the 1970s, the U.S. Treasury supplied a total of only 78 million ounces in bullion sales, most of it from coin-melt. It used a mere 12 million ounces for limited issues of part-silver coins. Meanwhile, foreign governments supplied 133 million ounces to the markets (also mostly from coin-melt) and used 295 million ounces for (mostly commemorative) coins.

World *mine production* of silver for the decade totalled 2.521 billion ounces, increasing from an annual rate of 252 million ounces in 1970 to 268 million ounces in 1979 (270 million ounces in 1980), *an average annual increase of .6 percent.* Additionally, commercial *secondary recovery* (salvage sales), including private coin-melting, totalled 666 million ounces for the decade, increasing from an annual rate of 30 million ounces in 1970 to 81 million ounces in 1979 (121 million ounces in 1980, with record prices), *an average annual increase of 17 percent.* Taken together, *total production* for the decade (mine and secondary) totalled 3.187 billion ounces, inceasing from an annual rate of 282 million ounces in 1970 to 349 million ounces in 1979 (391 million ounces in 1980), *an average annual increase of 2.3 percent.*

World *industrial use* of silver in the decade totalled 3.963 billion ounces, increasing from an annual rate of 339 million ounces in 1970 to 420 million ounces in 1979, *an average an-*

nual increase of 2.4 percent. Thus, the industrial use of silver was growing four times as fast as mine production, and a little faster than total production. World coinage use of silver in the decade[1] was 405 million ounces, declining from 38 million ounces in 1970 to 33 million ounces in 1979 (20 million ounces in 1980); however the potential exists for private and/or official use of silver for coinage to expand sharply in coming years as discussed earlier in Chapter III. *Industrial and coinage use* combined in the 1970s totalled 4.368 billion ounces, increasing from an annual rate of 377 million ounces in 1970 to 453 million ounces in 1979, *an average annual increase of 2 percent.*

Subtracting the total of mine production, salvage production and Far East export silver of 3.581 billion ounces, from total industrial and coinage consumption of 4.368 billion ounces, the gross deficit between total production and total consumption for the decade of the 1970s was .787 billion ounces.

This 787 million-ounce shortfall was covered as follows:

133 mil. oz. from foreign government bullion stocks
302 mil. oz. from foreign government coin-melting
 78 mil. oz. from U.S. Treasury bullion stocks
244 mil. oz. from net speculative sales
 30 mil. oz. reduction in user inventories

The charts that follow show graphically what happened in the world silver markets in the 1960s and 1970s, and approximately *what must happen* in the next few years. In the decade of the 1960s the shortfall between total consumption and total production was fully met by governments selling their silver stocks and coin melt. In the 1970's the shortfall was met by a combination of coin melting and a substantial **depletion** in privately held silver stocks. These supplies are now virtually exhausted.

In the decade of the 1980's the shortfall cannot be met. It cannot be met for even half of this decade!

It can be met for two years, through 1983, as it was met for the last three years, by speculatively held silver, only on the

---

[1]Excluding the U.S., which used only 12 million ounces (from residual U.S. Treasury stocks) in the 1970s, terminating in 1977.

Chart 13
Silver Production/Consumption Trends

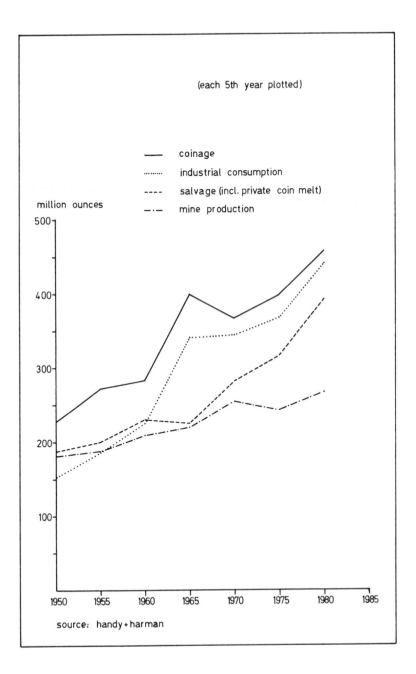

(each 5th year plotted)

—— coinage
.... industrial consumption
- - - - salvage (incl. private coin melt)
— · — mine production

million ounces

source: handy + harman

Chart 14
Silver Market Demands *

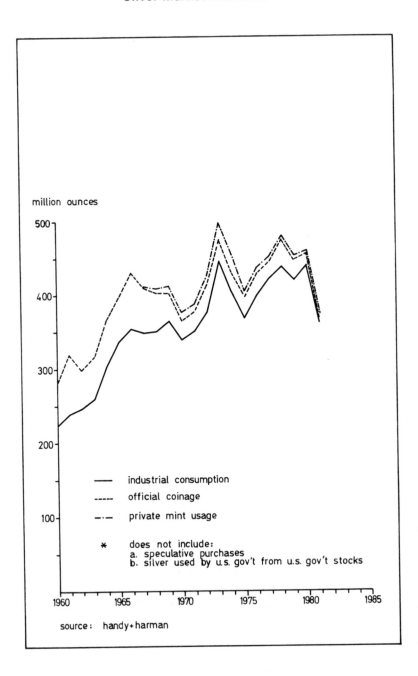

million ounces

500

400

300

200

—— industrial consumption

----- official coinage

—·— private mint usage

*   does not include:
a. speculative purchases
b. silver used by u.s. gov't from u.s. gov't stocks

100

1960   1965   1970   1975   1980   1985

source: handy+harman

assumption that the users bid high enough prices to draw out three fourths of the speculative stocks of silver in the world. By 1984, no matter what the users are willing to pay, there will have to be a sharp curtailment in consumption because *enough silver will not be available at any price!*

Chart 14 depicts industrial and coinage use by everyone *except the U.S. Government, whose full requirements in the period covered were met from Treasury stocks.*

Review of 1980/81

In their annual review of the silver market for 1981 (published early in 1982), Handy and Harman estimated 1981 *world industrial silver use* at 363 million ounces, up from 350 million ounces in 1980. At the same time, they estimated investments and speculative purchases of 49 million ounces (against the background of 116 million ounces of purchases in 1980). Our estimates are that industrial use was about 60 million ounces higher at about 423 million ounces and that investment and speculative purchases were about 60 million ounces less, i.e. that there were actually speculative sales of at least 11 million ounces.

Official coinage use for 1981 was estimated by Handy and Harman at 6 million ounces.

Private minting of coins and medallions in the U.S. in 1981 were estimated by Handy and Harman at 3.3 million ounces.

World mine production for 1981 was estimated by Handy and Harman at 264 million ounces. Handy and Harman reports on silver are issued in February of each year, before final statistics for the prior year have come in, and every year the previous year's estimates, sometimes three years, have been revised.

Secondary supplies were estimated in 1981 by Handy and Harman at 155 million ounces (foreign government bullion sales, 2 million ounces; officially demonetized coin, 12 million ounces; smuggled silver from the far east, 33 million ounces;

and 105 million ounces from industrial scrap and private coin melt salvage). Every category went down from 1980 — a trend we expect to continue this year. The reported 155 million ounces of total salvage in 1981, down from 223 million ounces in 1980, was motivated in part by low silver prices prevailing in 1981, but was also due to a point of diminishing return being reached and salvage recovery efforts. We do not expect that the 1980 record salvage amount of 223 million ounces will ever be reached again in this decade, because it was only achieved by cleaning out the buréau drawers everywhere of all odds and ends of silver flatware, serving dishes, unwanted jewelry pieces, etc, and those drawers must be virtually empty of such junk silver.

1981 total world supply and demand can be summarized from the foregoing as follows:

DEMAND

Industrial Usage	423 million ounces
Official Coinage Usage	6 million ounces
Private Mintage	3 million ounces
Investor Speculative Sales	(11) million ounces
Total Market Demand	421 million ounces

SUPPLIES

Mine Production	264 million ounces
Secondary Supplies	155 million ounces
Other	2 million ounces
Total Market Supply	421 million ounces

Chart 15 shows total market supplies *including* U.S. Treasury sales and silver certificate redemptions. It shows that

Chart 15
Silver Market Supplies *

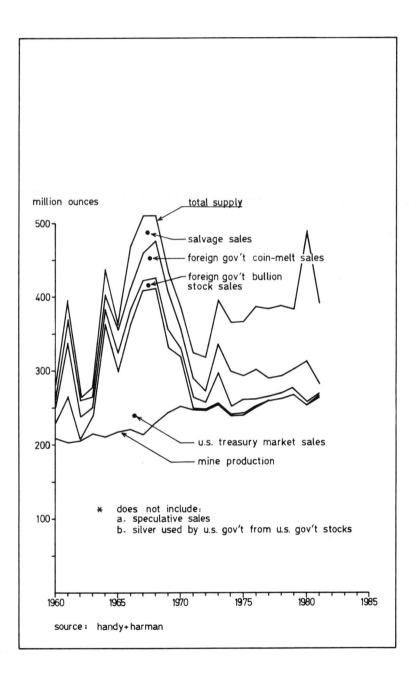

million ounces   total supply

500 —
                              ← salvage sales
                              ← foreign gov't coin-melt sales
                              foreign gov't bullion
                              stock sales
400 —

300 —

                              u.s. treasury market sales

200 —   mine production

        *   does not include:
100 —   a. speculative sales
            b. silver used by u.s. gov't from u.s. gov't stocks

1960   1965   1970   1975   1980   1985

        source :   handy+harman

Chart 16
Total Silver Market Supply, Demand & Price *

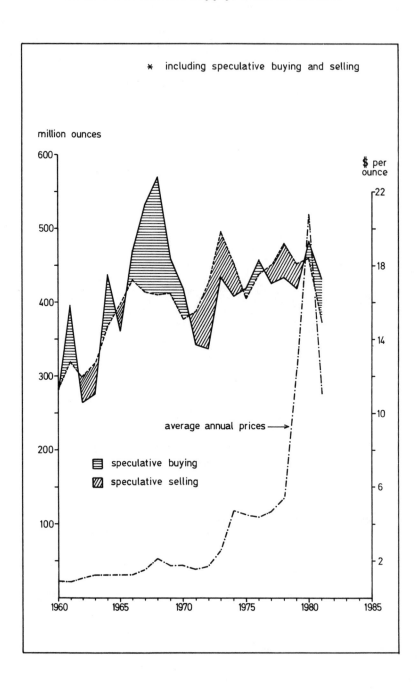

the Treasury *had been* overwhelmingly the dominant market supplier of silver in the decade of the 1960s. During the past decade, governments' demonetized coin and other salvage (secondary production) helped bridge the gap between new mine production and total consumption, the statistics clearly show that left-over silver bullion from former U.S. Treasury stocks held by the public, coin melt silver and stepped-up salvage recovery were important sources of supply.

Chart 16 is derived from the previous two charts. This chart depicts the total producer market supply plotted with total consumer market demand. Where the lines cross there is a balance. Where supply is more than demand the difference, by definition, is speculative purchases; and, conversely, where demand is more than supply the difference is speculative sales. From 1985 on there simply will not be enough silver available at any price for present consumer demand trends to continue. Once loose aboveground supplies are fully depleted, total producer supplies and total consumer demand must be brought together by prices well over $100 per ounce.

This forecast is based solely on supply/demand considerations and does not provide for the effect of a hyperinflationary scenario. Were gold to be officially or unofficially remonetized at say $5,000 (or $50,000), the silver price would also add one or two (or three) zeros to its paper-dollar price.

Preview of 1982/85

Taking the foregoing supply/demand discussion together with the federal government's penchant for creating ever more issues of inflationary paper money, there can remain little doubt that sometime in 1982 we will see the beginning of the major new multi-year rise in the price of silver. To recap what we have seen thusfar, there are four fundamental reasons:

1. Past price control. Past artificial elasticity of market supplies offered from U.S. Treasury stocks in the 1960's at controlled low prices, built up private stocks, discouraged production, and encouraged consumption in the 1970's. This form of price control had exactly the same bad effect as decreed prices, plus the further effect (because of the build up of private in-ventories) of continuing, for most of the 1970's, to artificially depress market prices long after direct official market sales had ceased. When this after-effect ends completely, the silver price will move **massively** in a direction opposite the control (up) to whatever level is required to ration grossly inadequate current supplies to (only) the most urgent demands.

2. Inelastic supply. 75% of the total annual world produc-tion of silver comes as a by-product of non-ferrous base metals, chiefly copper, lead and zinc. As a result, silver production cannot be much increased without causing prohibitive mining costs and over-production of these base metals. Supply is therefore extremely inelastic (i.e. insensitive to price changes.)

3. Inelastic demand. World industrial demand, for thou-sands of individually small but high-volume uses, is inelastic and price insensitive. This is so because most end-product items use such small amounts per unit produced that the cost of the silver per unit is a small percentage of the cost of manufacture, and because silver's several unique properties make it essential to many different industries — regardless of its price.

4. Shortage. The total annual world consumption of silver is almost 50% greater than the total annual world mine produc-tion, and the deficit is increasing as the long-term trend of in-creased consumption grows more rapidly than mine produc-tion. Private inventories (industrial and investment), earlier supplied by U.S. Treasury sales in the 1960 s, were above nor-mal levels in the 1970 s, near normal in recent years, and will be below normal by 1983 — forcing silver users to depend heavily on the little remaining investor-owned supplies avail-able, and also forcing them to curtail some areas of end use in 1984 and beyond.

In short, based upon each of the foregoing considerations, and in view of the 1980/81 price decline, silver prices in early 1982 are still artificially and heavily depressed. Today private inventories are less than a third of their level a decade ago, and silver, slightly under $10 per ounce as this is written, is presently the most under priced commodity in the world. And it will likely remain so through mid-1982. However, when the world's industrial users inventories are below normal levels (by 1983) and, for the first time ever they must try to buy their requirements in a completely unhampered market, silver prices will sail upward as never before.

Chart 17 illustrates our opinion of what the shortage and inelasticity factor's effects will be with price freedom on silver prices in 1983-85, *without considering the effects of much worse inflation or possible remonetization of silver.*

This chart illustrates the principle only. The details shown here as equal changes in price and quantity, in practice are usually not equal. They vary in relative magnitudes from one item to another—sometimes even for the same item at different times. (This graphic method of displaying the market impact of price changes was originated by the late Dr. F.A. Harper, founder of the Institute for Humane Studies, Menlo Park, California.)

There were speculative scrambles into silver in 1967-68, 1972-74 and 1977-79, each of which multiplied the silver price from two to four times. There will be another, more fervent, scramble beginning in 1982 that will carry the silver price to the $100 to $200 range by 1985.

When there is a resumption of high double-digit inflation (over 20 percent), then all of the values in the price column of Chart 17 would have to be increased accordingly. Obviously, it is not possible to predict a price change so accurately as a reading of this chart by itself would imply. We therefore simply say this: Without considering the effects of a substantial further depreciation of the dollar, we expect the price of silver to be in the $100-plus-per-ounce range by 1985. Each reader should form his own opinion and act on his own interpretation of the facts, his own judgment of the validity of the trend projections we have made, and his own opinion of what approximate price to expect during the period of his anticipated holding.

Taking the middle of our range, a $50 price in two years would amount to a 500 percent appreciation from the recent $10 price. It *could* be at that level in one year; it *could* take three years to reach that level. These projections could easily

Chart 17
Effects of Price Freedom

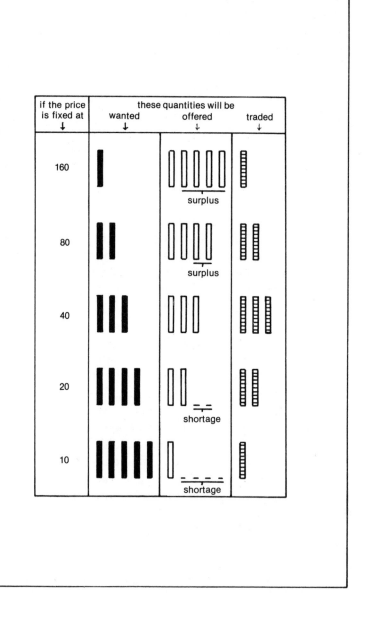

be off that much either way. (Or hyperinflation could add many zeros to these prices.)

Thus far, we have considered the outlook for silver based solely on the fundamental supply and demand factors. However, because of its historic relationship with gold as a monetary metal, a comparison of the price trends of both metals is revealing. Similarly, the third precious metal, platinum, is also related by its price movements to gold, although more tenuously.

We will analyze the price movements of all three metals in some detail in Chapter VIII, after we have examined the supply/demand fundamentals for gold and platinum in turn.

CHAPTER VI

Gold: The "Barbarous Relic"

Gold has always been . . . valued for its beauty, utility and durability. Today, it is more highly prized than ever, and its value will continue to rise according to the decline of fiat paper currencies.

. . .As fewer and fewer people have confidence in paper as a store of value, the price of gold will continue to rise.[1]

Unlike silver (or platinum) which can be studied on a supply/demand basis, there are more considerations and uncertainties involved when trying to formulate price projections for gold. Among them are the gold holdings of the world's central banks, which amount to about 1.1 billion ounces, just under one-half of the global stock of bullion. Even though gold has been "officially" demonetized, these central banks don't seem confident enough of that "fact" to sell off their holdings.

Another uncertainty in the supply side of the gold market equation is that the U.S.S.R. is the second largest producer of the metal, but mine production statistics are a closely guarded state secret.

We will first take a look at the more easily gathered demand data, before attempting to analyze gold supply figures.

Industrial and Commercial Demand

Because of the very high price of gold throughout most of 1980, commercial demand in all three of the major categories

---

[1]Jerome F. Smith, *The Coming Currency Collapse — And What You Can Do About It*, pp. 103, 104.

Chart 18
Gold Price In US$

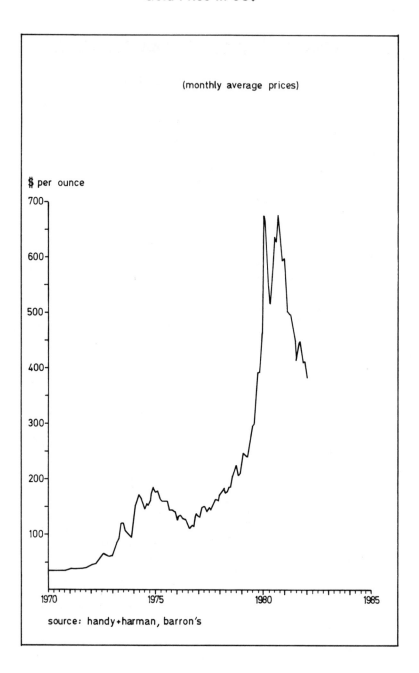

(monthly average prices)

$ per ounce

source: handy+harman, barron's

of gold use (jewelry and arts, dental and industrial) declined quite substantially. In the U.S., the largest decline was in the jewelry and arts category, from 2.6 million ounces used in 1979 to only 1.5 million ounces in 1980 — a drop of over one million ounces, largely due to the resistance of consumers to making purchases of jewelry at the higher price levels. The experience in the United States has been that retail demand for the very expensive high-quality items of jewelry does not fall nor do the very cheaply priced items in "discount" stores. The huge drop in sales occurred largely in the middle area of quality and price.

Uses for dentistry and industry dropped in the same period by 196,000 ounces (from 626,000 to 430,000) and by 344,000 ounces (from 1,401,000 to 1,057,000) respectively.

In spite of the huge drop in the price of gold during the first quarter of 1981, the only usage category which increased over the first quarter of 1980 was industrial, where the gold used is a tiny amount per unit of end product. Jewelry usage in the first quarter of 1981 was down a whopping 522,000 ounces under first-quarter 1980 (from 836,000 ounces to 314,000 pounces). The same effect was registered in the dental industry where consumption figures for first-quarter 1981 are only half what they were for the same period in 1980. Table IX depicts the precipitous drop in gold usage experienced in 1980 as a result of record high gold prices. Note the relatively unchanged demand in the years prior to the unprecedented 1979-80 rise of the gold price.

World Industrial Gold Demand

Visible in Chart 19 is the effect on worldwide commercial gold demand as a result of the higher gold prices in 1979-80. Jewelry and commemorative medals and medallions suffered

Table IX

U.S. Gold Consumption, 1970-81
(thousands of troy ounces)

	1970	1971	1972	1973	1974	1975	1976	1977	1978	1979	1980	1981*
Jewelry and arts	3340	4299	4344	3473	2402	2080	2562	2658	2651	2600	1517	314
Dental	658	750	750	679	509	595	694	656	706	626	430	62
Industrial**	1975	1884	2191	2577	1740	1059	1233	1205	1313	1401	1057	315
Total Usage	5973	6933	7285	6729	4651	3734	4489	4519	4670	4627	3004	691

*First-quarter figures.   **Including space and defense.
Source: Commodity Year Book, Commodity Research Bureau Inc. 1980 and first-quarter 1981 from Green's Commodity Market Comments.

Chart 19
World Industrial Gold Demand*

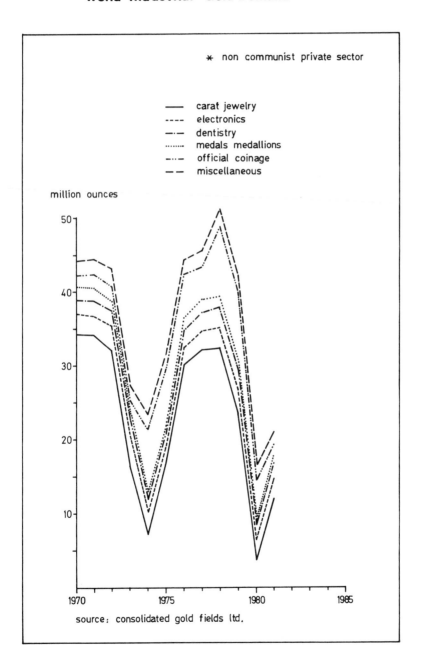

the most with a drop of 84 and 55 percent respectively in gold usage. The electronics industry used only 14 percent less, exhibiting the necessity of using gold in that field for applications where only minute quantities are employed per unit of end product. As with silver, demand for gold in electronics is vital where used and is relatively price insensitive in industry as a whole.

Interestingly, official gold coinage registered a drop of only 39 percent in usage over the same period (see Table X). Again, as with silver, it seems that official coinage of precious metals is *not* on the way out.

Although the dramatic changes in gold prices in 1980 caused some countries to defer the issuance of gold coins, 57 countries issued 176 different gold coinages during 1980 as reported in the new book, *Modern Gold Coinage—1980*, published by The Gold Institute.

In 1973, only six countries issued gold legal tender coins. In 1977 . . . the number of nations grew to 46, and to 57 in 1980. In 1977, 84 different gold coinages were issued, with 176 issues in 1980. Excluding the Krugerrand, in 1977, some 793,531 troy ounces of pure gold were used in the minting of other gold coins, but by 1980 . . . this usage in coins other than the Krugerrands had more than tripled to 2,619,318 troy ounces.[2]

Table X
Official Gold Coinage, 1976-80

Year	Nations Issuing	Ounces Used
1976	46	4,298,782
1977	46	3,629,750
1978	49	7,281,005
1979	80	9,905,274
1980	57	6,087,071

Source: The Gold Institute.

Gold Production

South Africa is by far the largest producer of gold in the world, accounting for about three-quarters of total produc-

---

[2]Excerpted from July 1981 issue of *The Gold News/Nouvelles de l'Or*. (Quoted by Mr. Richard L. Davies, Managing Director, The Gold Institute, Washington, D.C.)

tion. If political turmoil were to heat up in that part of the globe, a continuing possibility, there is no telling how much of, or how long, the world's supply would be interrupted from this major source of production.

Supplies from South Africa have declined dramatically in the last ten years from 32.16 million ounces in 1970 to only 21.70 million ounces in 1980. Production from other major producers of gold has also declined substantially in the same period. Canada, which produced 2.41 million ounces in 1970, produced only 1.59 million ounces in 1980, and the U.S.A. declined from 1.74 million ounces in 1970 to .86 million ounces in 1980.

Production in Latin America and Oceania, on the other hand, climbed in the last ten years, the former from 1.14 million ounces to 2.75 million ounces and the latter from .77 million ounces to 1.13 million ounces. Table XI gives the breakdown for gold production in the West during the 1970s, and Chart 20 shows total estimated gold supplies in the world.

Soviet sales to the West were quite small until 1972 when approximately 6.85 million ounces were released. U.S.S.R. gold sales rose in the period 1972 to 1976 to about 12.26 million ounces. They averaged that amount until 1979 when sales declined dramatically to 6.40 million ounces. Perhaps the declining production trend in gold is being experienced in Soviet Russia as we know it is in the rest of the world generally.

Between 1979 and 1980 the level of new production remained almost unchanged, declining slightly from 30.90 million ounces in 1979 to 30.31 million ounces in 1980. The overall trend for the past decade, however, has been down quite substantially from 40.95 million ounces in 1970.

Official and Private Gold Holdings

While gold production has declined somewhat, total gold supplies available to the private markets rose in 1979 and

Table XI
Gold Production, 1970-80
(Excl. Communist-dominated areas; millions of troy ounces)

	1970	1971	1972	1973	1974	1975	1976	1977	1978	1979	1980
South Africa	32.16	31.39	29.24	27.50	24.39	22.94	22.94	22.50	22.71	22.61	21.70
Other Africa	1.43	1.43	1.36	1.44	1.40	1.29	1.26	1.33	1.10	.91	.95
Canada	2.41	2.21	2.08	1.93	1.68	1.65	1.68	1.74	1.74	1.64	1.59
United States	1.74	1.49	1.45	1.16	1.13	1.04	1.04	1.03	.97	.97	.89
Latin America	1.14	1.10	1.12	1.13	1.19	1.34	1.77	1.80	2.02	2.14	2.75
Asia	1.06	1.09	1.05	.97	.89	.85	.87	.97	.99	.93	1.01
Europe	.24	.24	.42	.46	.37	.35	.37	.42	.40	.32	.29
Oceania	.77	.79	1.27	1.31	1.28	1.20	1.25	1.46	1.55	1.38	1.13
Total World Production	40.95	39.74	37.99	35.90	32.33	30.66	31.18	31.25	31.48	30.90	30.31

Data: Consolidated Gold Fields, Ltd.

Chart 20
Estimated Gold Supplies

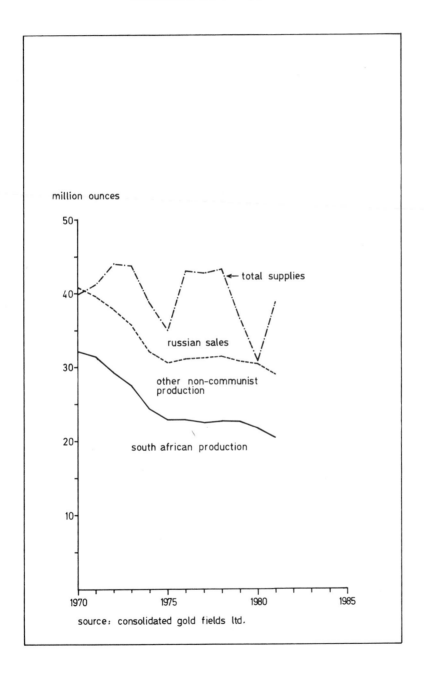

million ounces

total supplies

russian sales

other non-communist
production

south african production

source: consolidated gold fields ltd.

Chart 21
Soviet Gold Sales

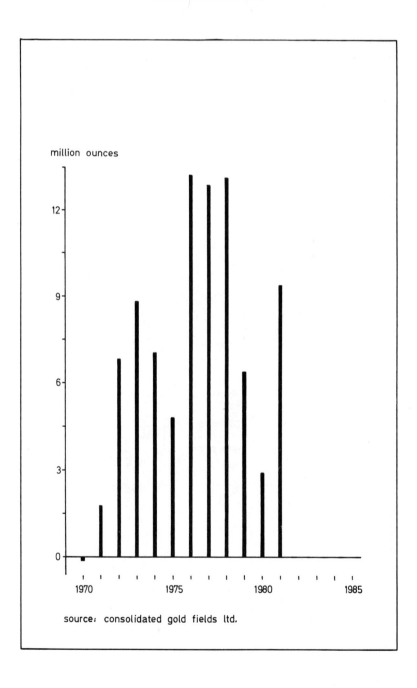

million ounces

source: consolidated gold fields ltd.

Chart 22
Official Gold Sales (+) Purchases (—), 1970-81

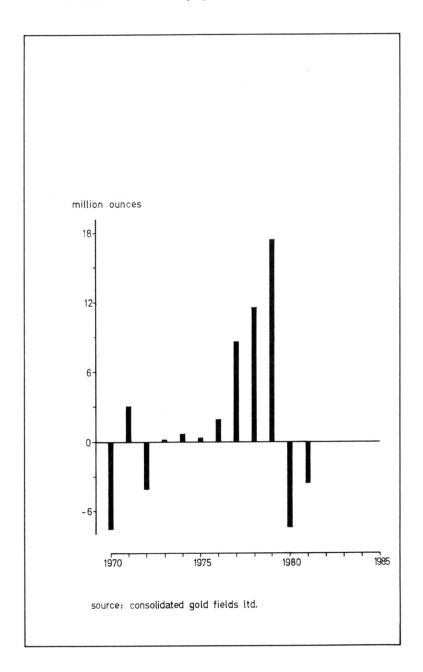

million ounces

source: consolidated gold fields ltd.

1980, entirely due to official (mostly U.S. Treasury) sales. Chart 22 displays the extent of official sales and purchases.

Table XII shows the official holdings of gold (and foreign exchange) as national monetary reserves for each country. As can be seen, the value of official gold is about four times greater than foreign exchange at market prices. Only Japan and Britain have less gold than foreign exchange.

Table XII
The West's Top Ten Gold-Holders

		Gold holdings*		
		at	at	Foreign
		SDR 35	market	exchange
	Million	per oz	prices **	holdings
	ounces	($Bil.)	($Bil.)	($Bil.)
United States	266.66	$12.1	$160.0	$ 4.8
W. Germany	118.64	5.4	71.8	34.9
France	101.99	4.6	61.2	8.3
Switzerland	83.28	3.8	50.0	13.1
Italy	83.13	3.8	49.1	13.8
Holland	54.78	2.5	32.9	3.1
Belgium	42.59	1.9	25.6	1.9
Japan	23.97	1.1	14.4	21.1
Britain	22.86	1.0	13.7	17.7
Canada	22.08	1.0	13.2	2.2
Total	819.98	$37.2	$491.9	$120.9

*For Belgium, Britain, France, West Germany, Holland and Italy — includes gold component of ecu holdings.
+ At $600 per ounce.
Source: World Market Perspective, Vol. XII, No. 12, Dec. 13, 1979.

Chart 23 displays the growth in bullion holdings by the private sector. Although there was a decrease of holdings in 1980, it only amounted to a 28 percent drop following a 1979 increase of 75 percent in private bullion accumulation.

Chart 23
Changes In World Fabricated and Bullion Holdings

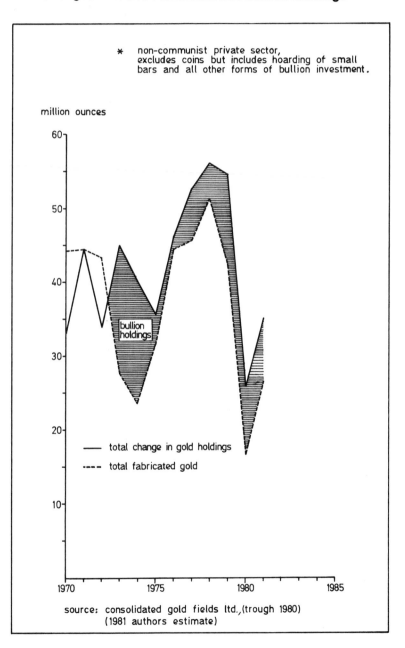

* non-communist private sector,
  excludes coins but includes hoarding of small
  bars and all other forms of bullion investment.

million ounces

bullion holdings

—— total change in gold holdings

---- total fabricated gold

source: consolidated gold fields ltd.,(trough 1980)
(1981 authors estimate)

Chart 24
Real Rates Of Return

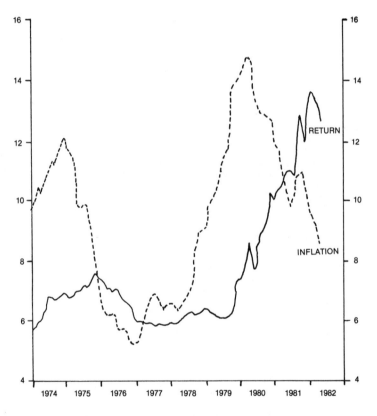

When real rates of return (the nominal rate minus the inflation rate) become negative, private investment in Gold is stimulated. Currently real rates of return are positive.

Source: Bache Halsey Stuart Shields.

Price Outlook

Even if commercial demand does not soon rise substantially, the effect of lower demand from this quarter could be offset by reduced official sales into the market. The only factor that could affect the overall supply outlook would be the resumption of substantial sales by the U.S. Treasury, which seems unlikely under the Reagan Administration. Further, with all the lip-service being paid to "going back to the gold standard," most countries, if not all, will be holding even more tightly onto the gold in their reserves. In spite of all of the rhetoric in the past about gold being a "barbarous relic," some decisive government officials apparently realize that ultimately the markets will decide what will be money — and what will not.[3]

The growing awareness of the effects of inflation on investments, and that none of the traditional forms of investment are as profitable or as safe as gold, is leading more and more people to hold gold as a real store of value for large amounts of capital. And as time goes on and more people become aware of the fact that interest-bearing investments are not usually keeping up with the rate of inflation and monetary depreciation, gold will gain more and more adherents. (40,000 ounces of gold was added to private U.S. investors' holdings in the first quarter of 1981.)

Of course whenever people believe — however mistakenly — that inflation is about to be brought under control from all of the rhetoric spewed out by politicians and the news media, the price of gold plummets. Such occasions should be viewed as bargain opportunities to buy gold. If it were true that inflation could be stopped, there would be no need to protect one's assets with gold or other hard-money investments. But the fact is, given the political context that exists today, that it is impossible for governments to stop inflating or even to have much success in reducing inflation for very long.

---

[3]"I don't think we should spend any time trying to fight gold or demonetize it, or bring down the price by dumping. We should thank our lucky stars we've got it." Henry Reuss, Chairman of the House Banking Committee (a long-time opponent of any role for gold in the monetary system), quoted in *Fortune*, November 5, 1979.

CHAPTER VII

Platinum: The Strategic Precious Metal

Compared to the principal precious metals, gold and silver, platinum's history is brief indeed. Traces of platinum have been found in unearthed decorative relics dating from ancient Egypt and Greece, but only in very minute quantities.

Platinum is the most familiar and most important member of a family of six metals with similar properties referred to as the "platinum group." The others, rarer, less used and less well known, are palladium, iridium, osmium, rhodium and ruthenium. Platinum and palladium comprise about 90 percent of the platinum-group metals.

As recently as 300 years ago, platinum was considered a nuisance when unearthed during gold-mining operations. It was discarded because it had no significant use in the culture or industry of that period. Platinum's first recorded modern use was in the early 1700s in Ecuador, where it was found in conjunction with the mining of gold. There was no other known use for the metal so it was employed in small amounts only for jewelry and decorative arts. And that remained its only significant, however minor, use for the next two centuries.

With the coming of age of modern technology — so too did the "noble white metal" (as it is sometimes called) come into its own and take its long-awaited place as a strategic and indispensable industrial commodity. The metal that had been scorned in past ages was "discovered," it seems, precisely in time for mankind to mechanize processes, computerize routine and take its first infant steps into outer space. Today, there is significant and growing demand for platinum.

Platinum Demand

In a very short time, platinum has moved out of research and development laboratories and into the industrial complex as a valuable catalyst for many different processes in industry. It is widely used in the chemical, electrical and petroleum industries, as well as in the space industry as a catalyst for fuel cell power supplies and as a protective coating for space vehicle surfaces. All of these industries are major suppliers both to other manufacturers and wholesalers generally, and to the aerospace/defense industry particularly.[1]

The recently renewed growth in defense spending and the burgeoning outer space program underway today augur well for platinum. The United States federal budget for fiscal 1982 allots $225.7 billion to aerospace and defense spending, a major part of which will go to companies in the above-listed industries. This indicates continued growth in the industrial use of platinum in this area.

In the past, Japan has been the largest consumer of platinum, and is also dependent on imports from other countries. Three-quarters of consumption is used in jewelry. The amount of platinum used for jewelry shows that the Japanese consider it a desirable component in their jewelry collections, whether it be simply for decoration or perhaps also for investment purposes. (In spite of the elimination of the outright ban on owning gold in Japan recently, there are still severe restrictions and penalties on unauthorized Japanese ownership of gold.)

By contrast, only 4 percent of U.S. consumption of platinum goes into jewelry. Western economies place a higher importance on the technical properties of platinum (high melting point, chemical inertness and resistance to oxidization). The newest, largest and most well-publicized use in recent years, of course, has been in the automotive industry in catalytic converter exhaust devices. These and other uses are shown in Table XIII.

Automotive — By far the most prominent use of platinum in the automotive industry has been as a catalyst for purification of exhaust gases used in conjunction with the emission-control

---

[1]Jerome F. Smith, *The Coming Currency Collapse*, p. 104.

Table XIII
U.S. Platinum Consumption, 1974-81
(thousands of troy ounces)

	1974	1975	1976	1977	1978	1979	1980	1981*
Automotive	350	273	481	354	597	803	517	115
Chemical	216	149	83	84	149	98	119	23
Dental & medical	26	17	27	27	44	27	26	6
Electrical	99	73	89	90	106	116	150	32
Glass	74	34	41	60	98	88	53	12
Jewelry & commemorative	23	23	23	34	25	27	51	13
Petroleum	139	108	59	74	108	170	58	41
Miscellaneous	17	21	46	64	66	78	58	15
Totals	944	698	849	787	1058	1407	1032	257

*First quarter. Source: U.S. Bureau of Mines

Note: Use by the aerospace/defense industry is not reported separately but is included in categories shown above.

devices required by the United States government on vehicles produced since 1974. This category has quickly become the largest area of domestic usage, accounting for 50 percent of total domestic industrial demand. Moreover, worldwide demand is expected to expand further, assuming other nations adopt platinum catalytic converters. Japan and several European nations seem committed to catalytic devices for at least the next few years.

Although demand in this category suffered a 36 percent drop in 1980 due to decreased auto sales, consumption will rise along with increased auto sales in 1982 and beyond. Usage in the auto industry will grow more slowly than in the past, however, due to the trend towards smaller engines and diesels. That demand will increase further now appears to be beyond doubt; world car production has risen sharply in the last few years with the exception of 1980, and is expected to reach 45 million units by 1990 according to an industry estimate. In our opinion, this prediction will be exceeded, and the role of platinum as a major component of car exhaust-control systems seems assured for the next 10-15 years.

The steady growth in car production must contribute to a strengthening of platinum prices, particularly in view of the latest development, a platinum-rhodium three-way catalyst, which eliminates hydrocarbon, carbon monoxide and nitrogen oxide in one operation, an improvement on all previous catalytic converters. The platinum used in these devices is technically recoverable but, as only a tiny fraction (about 1/10th) of an ounce goes into each converter, most of the platinum used in automobiles is not actually recovered.

Chemical — Because of platinum's unique catalytic capability, chemical inertness over a wide variety of temperature ranges, and high melting point ($1,769°C$), it is used as a catalyst in applications where one or more of these characteristics is necessary. It is employed in the processing of a wide range of chemicals and pharmaceuticals, as well as in nitric acid production, because it assures purity and resistance to corrosion. Its resistance to corrosive materials also makes it invaluable in laboratory and processing equipment in the chemical industry. Chemical industry usage of platinum has declined significantly since 1976 due to the introduction of catalysts using artificial zeolite[2] of which only small amounts are needed in comparison to the amounts of platinum required to achieve the same end result. The chemical industry currently consumes about 10 percent of total industrial demand.

Dental and Medical — Platinum is widely used in dentistry and medicine. Used in gold-based alloys it adds strength and improves the color of dental work. In medicine it is used in such devices as hypodermic needles, cautery points and cardiac pacemakers (another expanding application that is in its early stages of development).

Electrical — Innumerable uses for platinum fall under this category because of its twin characteristics of high conductivity and high melting point. It is widely used for plating contacts in relays, voltage regulators, meters, spark plugs, thermostats, furnace motor windings, etc., and in printed circuits, resistors and other electronic components. Its chemical inertness makes platinum a useful metal in the communications field because its surface does not oxidize and platinum-plated contacts in telephone equipment will not produce electrical "noise" for many years after installation.

The relatively new development of large electrochemical fuel cells as an emergency source of power, may generate a substantial demand for platinum in the future.

Glass — The glass and ceramics industry uses platinum as decoration for fine china and glass dinnerware. Because of its high melting point and because it has the same coefficient of expansion as glass, it is also used to line glass-melting furnaces, and the perforated plates from which molten glass is poured to produce glass filaments. One of the reasons platinum is so valuable to this industry is its ability to withstand high-temperature corrosive conditions with little wear and without contaminating the glass.

A relatively new but expanding use in this industry for glass filaments and, therefore, for platinum to produce the fila-

---

[2]A hydrous silicate that is analogous in composition to feldspar (a metallic mineral), occurring as a secondary mineral in cavities of lavas which can act as an ion exchanger or as a molecular sieve.

ments, has been sparked by the introduction and growing use of glass optic filaments. Thinner than a human hair, these filaments relay communications, television and computer data signals. May 11, 1977, saw the world's first full-scale light-wave communications system go into operation using one and one-half miles of underground cable made of glass fibers. This system, at AT&T in Chicago, carries voice, data and video signals on pulses of light to their destination. A single optical fiber can carry as many as 2,000 telephone circuits or 12 television channels over a distance of more than one kilo-meter, and Times Fiber Communications, Inc., plans to pro-duce fibers capable of carrying 30 channels at once over distances of up to three kilometers (1.8 miles). In the 1980s, because of lower cost, faster and better quality transmission and greatly reduced space requirements, glass cables may well substantially replace copper cables in high-density traffic re-quirements in the communication signal transmission in-dustries.

Platinum is also used in the manufacture of fiberglass, 70 percent of which is used in building insulation. Demand for this application will grow along with an upturn in housing starts.

Petroleum — Platinum's major use in the petroleum industry is as a catalyst in what is called the "reforming process," a pro-cedure employed (as an alternative to banned ethyl-lead) to upgrade the octane rating of gasolines. It is also used in lesser amounts as a catalyst in two other refining processes, hydro-cracking and isomerization. Demand by the petroleum in-dustry can vary sharply from year to year, since catalytic devices can be re-used many times before they become ineffec-tive. In addition, production of a new catalytic crack-ing/reforming facility requires a large initial outlay of platinum, but much less thereafter. In this context, the in-crease in refinery capacity for the late 1970s proved to be a significant demand factor. Usage in this area is expected to rise in conjunction with the expanded demand for unleaded gasoline in the future.

Jewelry—As mentioned earlier, jewelry presently accounts for only 4 percent of platinum consumption in the United States. However, there are various advertising campaigns going on from time to time, financed by Rustenburg and other producers and sponsored by jewelers and refiners, to boost the popularity of platinum jewelry. This effort has already had an impressive success and can be expected to continue to do so.

Before World War II, platinum was highly regarded and valued by the very rich for jewelry, but with the advent of the war, it was put to use in aircraft engines and the like. This lessened its appeal in the eyes of many, who apparently were disinclined to associate an industrial commodity used in airplanes with fashionable jewelry. It is possible that these campaigns will spark more of an interest in this long-neglected, beautiful metal and increase the use of platinum by the jewelry industry in this country. Indeed, consumption in this area almost doubled from 1979 to 1980, the first time such a jump has occurred. And first-quarter 1981 consumption figures for the jewelry industry are very much higher than in the same period of 1980 (13,464 ounces in 1981 compared to 8,429 for 1980).

Private Coinage Demand—Most commemorative pieces struck, of course, are silver or gold; however, commemorative platinum medals and coins have been issued from time to time on a limited basis.

Franklin Mint and other producers of precious metal medallions and coins sell their commemorative pieces at a high premium price (above their metal-content value). Their markets could be greatly expanded and their pricing problems simplified if they emulated the South African government's pricing method for the very successful Krugerrand. Instead of advertising a high unit price (at the time of issue) which later becomes too low because of a surge in metal prices, they should settle for a less exorbitant margin. It should be stated candidly and prominently what the precious metal content is of each issue struck. They should also competitively price each piece at 2 or 3 percent above its metal value on the basis of closing metal market prices on the day an order is received.

If this practice becomes industry-wide, as we believe it will, the use of all the precious metals by private minters, and their market demands for these metals will soar.

Production of Platinum

Platinum production is limited to only a few countries, and the supply to Western industrialized nations is by no means guaranteed, when one considers that the world's two main producers are South Africa and the Soviet Union.

In the early 1800s, major deposits of platinum were discovered in Russia's Ural Mountains. A discovery in 1914 at Sudbury, Ontario, Canada, positioned that country to become the poor third largest producer of platinum-group metals. In 1924, large and rich deposits were found in the Merensky Reef located in the Bushveld Complex of South Africa, leading to that country becoming the world's largest producer of platinum. The possibility exists, however, that Russia is actually the world's largest producer of the metal. It is difficult to be certain because statistics from Communist-bloc countries are unverifiable.

Three large companies account for most of the mine production of the platinum-group metals outside the U.S.S.R. These companies produce about 95 percent of the platinum-group metals in the market economies. In the Republic of South Africa, Rustenburg Platinum Mines, Ltd., accounts for about two-thirds of South African output. It operates several mines in western Transvaal in two sections of the western arm of the Merensky Reef, and is developing a third section. . . . Impala Platinum Ltd. began production in 1969 and operates the Bafokeng and Wildebeestfontein mines at Rustenburg. . . . The International Nickel Co., Inc. (INCO) of Canada is the third-largest producer. It operates Canadian nickel mines at Sudbury, Ontario, and at Thompson, Manitoba, from which platinum-group metals are obtained as by-products.

The U.S.S.R. is the major world palladium producer and is also an important source of the other metals of the group. Little information has been published on production of the platinum-group metals in the U.S.S.R., and only estimates are available. Probably 95 percent of the output is a by-product of nickel-copper mining. . .

In addition to these major sources, there are a few lesser producers. In South Africa, Western Platinum Ltd., which began production in 1971 . . . Atok Platinum Mines Ltd., which began operation in 1969 . . . In Canada, Falconbridge Nickel Mines, Ltd., is second in importance to INCO.[3]

Table XIV identifies the geographical areas in which platinum is mined, and the amounts reported from each major producing nation.

Table XIV
World Production of Platinum, 1975-80
(thousands of troy ounces)

	1975	1976	1977	1978	1979	1980
South Africa	1838	1720	1720	1680	1765	2044
U.S.S.R.	700	720	605	575	500	334
Canada	180	230	170	140	130	174
Others	45	40	35	40	40	30
Total Production	2763	2710	2530	2335	2435	2582

Source: W.I. Carr Sons & Co., London. 1980 figures: preliminary estimate by J. Aron Precious Metals Research Department.

It is noteworthy that South Africa was able to double her production of platinum in only two years (1972-74) in direct response to advance notice of the projected needs of the American automotive industry for platinum-based catalytic converters to meet 1974 U.S. government emission control standards. Only South Africa could do this because the only primary platinum mines in the world are in South Africa. All other platinum production comes as a by-product of mining gold, nickel and copper ores.

The United States, which normally consumes between one-quarter and one-third of world mine production and imports about 99 percent of its supply of primary metal, is, with respect to the platinum-group metals, vulnerable to the actions of foreign governments. Although the

---

[3]W.C. Butterman, *Mineral Facts and Problems*, U.S. Bureau of Mines.

United States has sizable resources of platinum-group metals, they are undeveloped, poorly defined, and mostly subeconomic. Domestic mine supply currently is negligible compared with domestic consumption, and could not be increased quickly if foreign supplies were cut off.[4]

In 1980, 95 percent of platinum mine production came from U.S.S.R. and South Africa. Most of the other 5 percent came from Canada. Canada has the capacity to generate up to 15 percent of "normal" world supplies. However, due to reduced nickel output, Canada's platinum production has been below normal capacity. Even so, it did register a 26 percent year-to-year increase in production for 1980, while the U.S.S.R.'s exports were curtailed 34 percent over 1979 (this may or may not be a result of lowered mine production). South African production also increased in 1980, up 14 percent over 1979. J. Aron & Co. analysts are projecting a 10 percent rise in world mine production for 1981.

Secondary Supplies

Since the United States produces very little platinum domestically, and is a major industrial consumer, it must import most of the metal it uses. More than 90 percent of the United States' imports of refined platinum comes from South Africa and Britain. (Britain imports its ores from South Africa.) Any aggravation of the precarious situation in South Africa could result in an embargo, work stoppages and perhaps even a shutdown of mine operations there, leaving the United States heavily dependent on the U.S.S.R. for its supply of newly mined platinum. (And, the U.S. does not have any large stocks of platinum, as it has gold,to draw upon in the event of a disruption of import flows.)

If that unfortunate development occurs, the United States would have to slash its usage dramatically. It would be totally dependent on the small amount it imports from Canada via Britain (under 100,000 ounces),[5] the tiny amount produced

---

[4]W.C. Butterman, *Mineral Facts.*

[5]The platinum produced in Canada is a by-product of nickel mining which was cut back sharply in 1977 because of a glut in nickel inventories and new nickel production flows from non-platinum-bearing ores abroad.

domestically (2,000 ounces), that recovered from scrap and the normal amount recovered by refiners (all of which together would be less than 20 percent of its needs). Possible, but uncertain, future imports from the Soviet Union would be the only other source of supply.[6]

Table XV
Platinum Recovery in the United States
1975-1980
(troy ounces)

	From Scrap	From Refiners
1975	103,623	5,292
1976	64,901	2,748
1977	50,838	831
1978	75,585	1,081
1979	75,038	1,980
1980	154,075	535

Source: U.S. Bureau of Mines

Almost 95 percent of the platinum contained in scrap can be recovered; however, the problem is that most of the platinum recovered by U.S. industry comes from *processing the imported platinum from South Africa.* In the absence of this important flow the potential recovery total in the future would be a small fraction of the scrap amounts recovered by industry in recent years. Although world secondary production from recycled scrap jumped over 50 percent from 1979 to 1980, J. Aron & Co. are estimating a similar *drop* in supplies of platinum from that source for 1981. Total supplies are expected to rise in 1981 due to increased mine output. However, industrial demand, which declined during 1980, is expected to rise substantially in 1981, creating a global stock deficiency somewhere near 100,000 ounces. Most of the small amount of platinum recovered by refiners in the U.S. comes from refining copper ores which contain traces of platinum.

---

[6]The only additional source of platinum recovery is that found in spent nuclear fuels. However, at present it is not economically feasible or even possible to extract platinum from that source.

Political Factors
Affecting Supplies

In his well-documented book, *The War on Gold*, Professor Antony Sutton concludes that a soon-forth-coming military war in the decades-long east-west ideological war, will see either the Soviets or the U.S. invading South Africa, either directly or through hired pawn nations; the pretext will be to end apartheid, but the real object will be control of that "geographical freak's" vast mineral resources. Others, including ourselves, have earlier reached much the same conclusion.

If this conclusion is correct, and especially if the Soviets out-maneuver the U.S. in southern Africa, which now seems likely, the consequent absence of South Africa mineral exports from world trade would drive the prices of all of those minerals up almost instantly. The metal that would surge highest in price as a direct result, in our opinion, is platinum. Further, as one of the three principal precious metals, platinum in recent years has tended to follow gold and silver in price; it is thus a hedge against both war *and* inflation, even perhaps more so than gold, because of the absence of any existing large stockpiles of platinum.

Price Outlook

Platinum is such a rare and precious metal that it once traded at more than $200 an ounce over gold; indeed, in March of last year, platinum changed hands at over $1,000 an ounce, the Muhammed Ali (in terms of box office appeal) of the metals. Along with all precious metals, however, it fell in the face of slow economic activity, high interest rates and a strong dollar.[7]

Platinum is bought, sold and priced in three different ways. First, there is the primary or producer market. This refers to metal sold by the major South African and Canadian pro-

[7]*Barron's*, June 22, 1981, p. 52.

ducers totheir regular customers. Next is the dealer or spot market. Main participants in this market include: the Soviet Union, scrap dealers, small mines, and industrial and non-industrial users. Finally, platinum is traded on the New York Mercantile Exchange, the London Platinum Market, among the banks in Zurich and on exchanges in other major cities in Europe.

In the short term and, to a degree, in the intermediate term, the approximate level of platinum's price is set by the major producers. However, over periods of a year or more, especially since 1970, platinum has generally moved in tandem with silver and gold, reflecting the depreciation of "floating" currencies, particularly the U.S. dollar, and this tendency can be expected to continue. However, if there were to be either a sharp jump in platinum usage or a sudden curtailment of supplies reaching the markets, we could expect a correspondingly greater surge in platinum prices. Either, or *both, is a definite possibility.*

A study by General Electric estimated total unmined platinum in the world as of 1977 to be 299 million ounces, which is about *20 times smaller than the estimated unmined gold reserves.* Additionally, since the beginning of recorded history, 3,000 million ounces of gold have been mined, more than two-thirds of which still exists as bullion kept in various bank vaults in private and government stockpiles. Platinum, on the other hand, has only been mined in total, to date, to the extent of 41 million ounces, *75 times smaller than the total amount of gold mined.* And, each year virtually the entire new increment of mine production is consumed by industry. Consequently, platinum is much more scarce, potentially as useful industrially, and therefore potentially much more valuable, ounce-for-ounce, than is gold. Logically it appears that this must eventually be reflected to some substantial degree, at least in its price relative to gold.

> Even if the environment for precious metals remains inhospitable, platinum's strong industrial base, its high-technology applications which effectively bar substitutability, and its strategic importance in our era of rising military expenditures seem likely to guarantee that this metal's price will follow an upward trend.[8]

---

[8] J. Aron & Co., quoted in *Barron's*, June 22, 1981, p. 54.

Chart 25
Platinum Price *

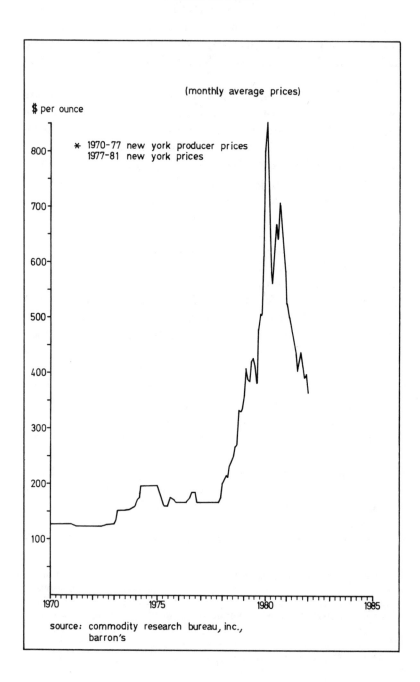

(monthly average prices)

$ per ounce

* 1970-77 new york producer prices
1977-81 new york prices

source: commodity research bureau, inc.,
barron's

Platinum's price over a period of months is largely subject to market supply and demand factors and over a period of years to its cost of production. But, as mentioned earlier, it has also tended to move in tandem with gold and silver in recent years.

The price of platinum had been relatively depressed in the past year (1981) along with gold and silver. However, on three notable occasions it moved well above the gold price, to over $900 per ounce. This happened in the months following the dollar crisis of 1968, again briefly in March of 1974, and in March of 1980 when it reached $1,000 per ounce (See Chart 28).

Since the number of producers of platinum is quite limited, the Soviets are able to exert considerable control at present on the price — expanding their exports only when world prices are acceptable (and they happen to need foreign currency credits to buy agricultural products from abroad), and exporting only minute quantities, or none at all when world prices are unacceptable (and/or they have had a good growing season). The price action in the past has reflected these uncertainties and has been both volatile and unpredictable in the short term, as can be seen in Chart 25 covering the period 1970 to date.

The long-term trend is unmistakably up and any one or more of the contingencies we've discussed can, and at some point will, cause future surges well above the gold price, again and again as has happened in the past. There is further the prospect that a future surge will permanently move the level of platinum prices above the price level of gold.

CHAPTER VIII

Silver, Gold and Platinum Price Movements Compared

The demands made and the supplies offered determine the price, the profits and the distribution.

The *economic value* of a thing is based upon usefulness and scarcity over time. The *market value* of a thing depends upon the amount of demands *made in the market*, and the amount of supplies *offered in the market* in a given period. The price, *in a free market*, is whatever it has to be to bring buyers and sellers voluntarily to trade an *equal* quantity at any given point in time.

Over a period of time, average price levels influence not only the amounts offered and demanded, but also the amounts produced and consumed. Price is the great equalizer that brings all other economic factors into harmony, rationing—always scarce—supplies to the most urgent market demands.

As we saw in Chapter V, there are several reasons to expect that in the case of silver, large increments of price increase will be required to effect the economically imperative equalization of consumption and production in the future. In addition, an analysis of silver's present price in conjunction with the price of gold provides further support.

Silver and Gold Supplies

In recent years (1976-80) annual world silver mine production has averaged 262 million ounces and gold mine production 30 million ounces. On this basis—without, for the moment, considering relative consumption rates or other factors—this 8.7-to-1 ratio would indicate a silver price of over 10 percent of the dollar gold price. Additionally, only about 60 percent of annual world gold mining production is used for industrial purposes while nearly 150 percent of the amount of annual world silver mine production is used for industrial purposes. This would seem to indicate a future silver price much higher in relation to gold than has been seen in many centuries.

Yet instead of being at a price ratio of 8.7 to 1 or even 16 to 1 (the former monetary ratio), recently silver has been at a price ratio to gold of about 40 to 1 (see Chart 26 on p. 123). Why? there are many minor contributing factors, but the main reason is that discussed earlier: government dumping of over one-and-one-half billion ounces of silver into private markets in the past two decades. This amount was not only enough to satisfy the production shortfall in the 1960s and 1970s, but it created a residual "overhang" of excess silver in private coin and bullion inventories of over a billion ounces early in the last decade. Depressed market prices (relatively) from 1970-77 were a direct result of this carry-over of excess silver.

The Gold/Silver Ratio

The coins were now establishing themselves in three classes: gold for governments and the wealthy, silver for merchants and their trade, and copper, brass, or bronze for the day-to-day needs of ordinary people. . . Croesus, King of Lydia, coined his gold and silver in a fixed value ratio, and this idea was continued. It was important that it should. With gold coins the nominal and intrinsic values were normally (in the absence of debasement or clipping) the same, but with silver the nominal value was usually considerably more than the intrinsic, a state of affairs which reaches its peak with paper money. Any overproduction of these soon begins to depreciate the real value of the currency in question and to inflate the local prices for goods.

The gold-silver ratio therefore provided a means for checking an excess of silver coin and restraining inflation. Soon after Rome started coining, the ratio settled down in the neighborhood of 1 (for gold): 10 (for silver), and it is a most astonishing thing that, with all the fluctuations in supply and world trade, it was still 1:11 in 1492; even by 1760 it had only moved to 1:14, and by 1860 to 1:15. Much has been written about this ratio and the factors that caused temporary and local movements in it, but yet on the whole kept it so relatively stable for so long a time.[1]

In 1968, when there was a free market in both gold and silver for a brief time and Treasury silver sales had not yet oversupplied the market, the historic price ratio of 16 to 1 between silver and gold reasserted itself. This happened again briefly at the price peaks in January 1980. A return to the 16-to-1 ratio in 1983-85 with gold at, say, $2,000 would put the silver price at $125.

Each person can draw his own conclusion about the significance of the historic silver/gold monetary link. We make these observations.

(1) Both gold and silver emerged in markets as money and served as money, by weight, long before any government put an imprint on either metal.

(2) The 16-to-1 ratio, or close to that, held from the 4th century B.C. until the last quarter of the 19th century — over 2,000 years.

(3) Less than one year after silver was set free in May 1967, gold also had to be set free (March 1968).

(4) The markets quickly adjusted to the 16-to-1 ratio when gold was set free in 1968, and again in 1980.

(5) It took a combination of massive government silver sales (over 1½ billion ounces) in the 1960s and a freeze on gold sales (March 1968) to depress silver prices, distorting the ratio for an entire decade thereafter.[2]

Throughout the 1970s there was an annual flow onto the markets of 30-50 million ounces of coinmelt silver, totaling 666 million ounces. Then, with the fantastic 1979-80 runup of silver prices, from under $20 per ounce in a few months to the

---

[1]Donald McDonald, "The History of Silver," *Silver: Economics, Metallurgy and Use*, (D. Van Nostrand Co. Inc., Princeton, N.J.). See Appendix A.

[2]U.S. Treasury silver sales were continued years after the coin shortage ended because Treasury officials knew that sacrificing their silver was the only way they could restrain the free market gold price without quickly losing their official gold. In so doing they distorted the silver/gold price ratio to more than 32 to 1.

January 1980 record high of $48 per ounce, another 121 million ounces was pulled into the markets when the large masses of the public dumped whatever unwanted household silver they could find. The 1960s, 1970s and 1979-80 silver supply events we've just described are all one-time, non-repeatable events.

In late 1979 and well into 1980, the long-term tendency for silver to be less volatile than gold was disturbed by two unprecedented actions by market professionals discussed in detail in Chapter II. First, driving silver prices up, were the massive pyramiding purchases by the Hunt family beginning about mid-1979—financed again and again in the rising market by the Hunts borrowing heavily against many tens of millions of ounces already held, to buy more tens of millions of ounces. This, added to other feverish buying, rocketed the silver price from about $17 per ounce to almost $50 in only a few months leading to January 1980.

The second unprecedented action was by officials of the (futures market) commodity exchange, who suddenly changed the rules, prohibiting new purchases while continuing to allow new sales transactions to be entered. The predictable effect was to force a precipitous fall in the silver price in the early months of 1980.

As a result of these extreme actions, silver for a short time was more volatile than gold. In the second half of 1979, the Hunts massive purchases caused silver to become overvalued in relation to gold; in the first half of 1980, the exchange officials' precipitous action caused the opposite to occur and silver has become even more undervalued in relation to gold in 1981, due, we believe, to the mass of the public having been temporarily scared away from participation in silver trading by the extreme silver price volatility in the 1979-80 period. These recent extreme divergences in relative gold and silver prices can readily be seen in Chart 26.

This chart displays two distinct longer-term trends. From mid-1968 through 1973, a period during which there was a large overhang of officially supplied silver, gold trended up at a higher rate than silver and the ratio therefore moved up. Then, from the beginning of 1974 to early 1980, as

Chart 26
Gold/Silver Ratio

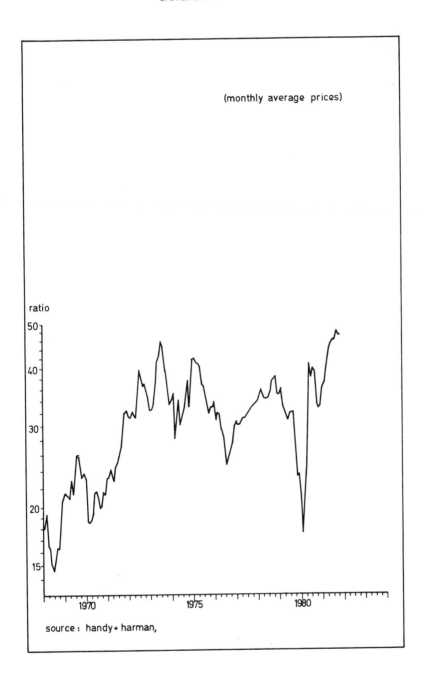

(monthly average prices)

ratio

source : handy + harman,

aboveground stocks of silver steadily diminished, the trend favored silver and the ratio generally declined. We believe the extreme divergences in the 1980-81 period, first favoring silver, then gold, have not signalled any change in the longer-term trend favoring silver since 1973. We believe silver will generally move up at a higher percent rate of increase than gold in the future as aboveground silver stocks fall farther.

We believe that the Hunt massive pyramiding (driving prices up) and the unprecedented and highly unprincipled exchange officials' rule-changes—the foolish actions that distorted the ratio in late 1979-early 1980 and which, in the aftermath, relatively depressed silver all through 1981—are most unlikely ever to be repeated in the future. One reason is the object lesson learned on both sides. The Hunts and other "longs" were obviously damaged, but so were the exchange officials thereafter because their precipitous action sent exchange customers away in droves.

We expect that the presently depressed ratio (against silver) is an after-effect that will be corrected to a more normal one in the '82-'83 period, with silver continuing to rise more than gold thereafter.

Another informative indicator of the direction of silver prices is the relationship between the exchange warehouse stocks of silver and silver prices. As discussed in Chapter IV, there has most usually been an inverse relationship, i.e., when stocks fall, prices rise—and vice versa.

Most quarters in which the silver stock declines are usually followed by a quarter of higher prices. Multiple-quarter drops in stocks are usually harbingers of substantial two-to-three year dollar-price uptrends and a favorable trend (for silver) in the ratio.

Gold and Platinum Prices

There are also some interesting and useful patterns observable in comparing gold prices with platinum prices. In the past decade, platinum has usually been higher in price than gold. However, there have been repeated short periods when the platinum price has gone lower than gold with both at depressed levels. In the last two bull markets in precious metals, platinum went to a substantial premium over gold. These relationships are evident in Chart 27, which shows the prices of gold and platinum together.

On those rare occasions when platinum is at a discount to gold, and one or the other is to be purchased at the beginning (or in anticipation) of a major rise—the best choice in the past two cycles has been platinum, and one can expect this to be the case in the future.

Silver, Gold and Platinum

Since 1972 all of the precious metals have tended to have about the same long-term rate of gain. For example, compare the gain from January 1973 with gold at $65 per ounce and silver at $2.00 per ounce, to September 1980 with gold at $666 and silver at $20.50. The difference in the gain between the two metals was less than 1 percent.

For the small investor, or anyone who wants to own only one precious metal, silver is the outstanding choice—especially at recent price levels. Larger portfolios should contain all three precious metals for diversification. Even though all three tend to move in tandem over any substantial period, they diverge from one another for shorter periods—sometimes quite dramatically, as we have seen. This argues for diversification as a means of lessening the price volatility of one's precious metals portfolio, especially one's core holdings (i.e., the fully paid, long-term portion one intends to hold through thick and thin until some viable alternative to today's unsound paper money emerges).

Chart 27
Gold Vs. Platinum Prices

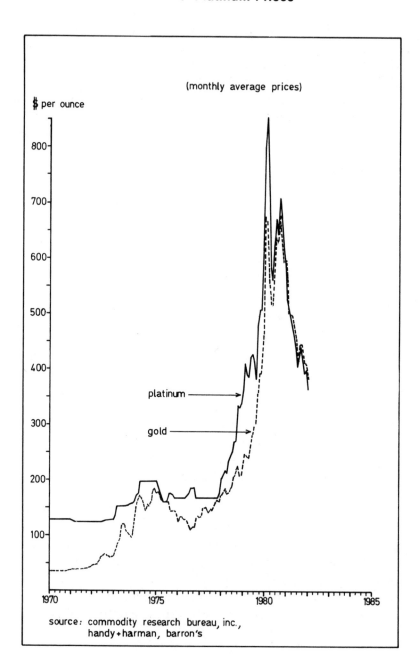

(monthly average prices)

$ per ounce

platinum

gold

source: commodity research bureau, inc.,
handy+harman, barron's

Chart 28
Gold, Silver and Platinum Prices

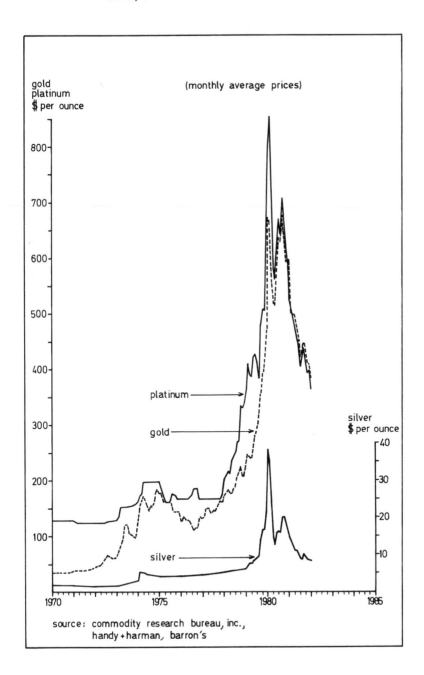

gold
platinum
$ per ounce

(monthly average prices)

platinum
gold
silver

silver
$ per ounce

source: commodity research bureau, inc.,
handy+harman, barron's

The relative volatility of these metals also argues for selectivity amongst the three, depending upon their relative prices at any given time. This is especially so for increments of purchase (or sale) which are above the basic core holdings.

CHAPTER IX

Inflation and the Monetary Metals

Gold and silver are monetary metals. They have been for at least six thousand years, since recorded civilization began. It is true that for a relatively short time (three decades), just before and after the turn of this century, a gold standard formally replaced the bi-metallic standard which had preceded it for thousands of years. But silver continued to be used in full-weight silver dollars and in subsidiary coinage after the gold standard was compromised in World War I and modified in the 1920s and even long after it was abandoned in the '30s. Because both are money metals the prices of these two metals in terms of the U.S. dollar has always tended to move in tandem over a period (e.g., the 1970s). This demonstrates to us that people regard both gold and silver as money today, just as they always have. In the long term, people — not governments or nation-states — determine what money is.

The Remonetization of Gold and Silver

One of the functions of money is as *the means of final payment*. The recent actions of certain central banks in using their gold as collateral for international loans — *pledging it as the means of final payment* — show that they implicitly recognize gold as the final and true international money. The world's central bankers, by resolutely hoarding their gold, are demonstrating that they also believe gold to be the means of final payment — in short, that gold is money. All other instruments they deal with inbetween — the "SDR", the U.S. dollar and other national currencies, are all in reality only I.O.U.s for gold. These I.O.U.s are presently in default. They will eventually either pass out of existence or again become redeemable in gold or silver at a small fraction of their former value, i.e., with a large multiple increase to a new official gold price, as compared to whatever the free-market price may be at the time such a move is made — if it is made.

It is not commonly understood that, even at $850 per ounce (the 1980 high), gold had gone nowhere near as high as it would have to in order to fully reflect the paper-money inflation which has occurred in the last four decades. Eventually, sooner or later, it will do just that. How high would it have to go to do this? And, a like question, how high would it have to be pegged, in an "official return to a gold standard," in order to function as intended for a time (until the whole inflationary scenario began again as it did in the early part of this century)?

Our good friend George Reisman has done an interesting examination of these questions. His analysis and projections follow. His conclusions, in percentage-price-increase terms, in our judgment apply even more forcefully to silver.

What Price Gold? [1]

" While inflation raises the price of gold, it does not, by itself, raise the price of gold relative to the prices of other things. But the demand for gold as an inflation hedge does raise the price of gold relative to prices in general. If one wants to form a meaningful estimate of the potential price of gold, it is the influence of the inflation hedge demand that one must consider. For inflation by itself will almost certainly raise the price of gold to tens of thousands,

[1]This section was written by Professor George Reisman for the July 1980 issue of *World Market Perspective* and is included with permission.

millions, and even billions and trillions of dollars an ounce; but it will also raise the price of cigarettes, a loaf of bread, and a pair of shoes by a similar order of magnitude. If one wants to estimate the potential buying power of an ounce of gold, one must momentarily ignore the influence of inflation itself and focus on the influence of the inflation-hedge demand in isolation.

Such an estimate can be formed by imagining that across the world the point is reached where people, on the average, wish to hold, say, ten or, alternatively, twenty percent of the value of their accumulated savings in the form of gold—figures which do not seem at all unreasonable in view of gold's qualities as an inflation hedge. Given these percentages, what we need to know to estimate the potential buying power of an ounce of gold is the total monetary value of accumulated savings in the world and the total quantity of gold in the world available for holding.

The total monetary value of accumulated savings in the world can be estimated by starting with the U.S. GNP (a concept that is objectionable in many respects, but which nonetheless has some valuable applications). Currently [Spring 1980], the GNP was running at about a $2.5 trillion annual rate. Historical statistics show total accumulated savings in the U.S.—the total value of factories, mines, farms, stores, urban land, houses, and the like—to run on the order of four times GNP. The American GNP is estimated to represent roughly one-fourth of the world GNP. If we allow for historically lower levels of savings relative to GNP in most countries compared with the U.S., and for a substantial reduction in the U.S. ratio as well, because of inflation, we might estimate the world total of accumulated savings at $20 trillion. This figure results from multiplying the U.S. GNP by 4, to arrive at world GNP, and then multiplying by 2 (instead of 4) to obtain a more conservative ratio of accumulated savings to GNP.

The world stock of gold is most commonly estimated to be between two and three billion ounces. Of this total, central banks are known to hold approximately 1.1 billion ounces. Assuming that the central banks will not wish to significantly reduce their holdings, this leaves between one and two billion ounces of gold available for private holdings.

If two billion ounces is the amount of gold available for private holdings, ten percent of the accumulated world savings in the form of gold would imply a price of gold of $1,000 per ounce in 1980 dollars. At the upper extreme, if one billion ounces is the amount of gold available for private holdings, twenty percent of accumulated world savings in the form of gold would imply a price of $4,000 per ounce in 1980 dollars. (In subsequent years, as inflation continues and GNP rises, these figures would, of course, have to be revised steadily upward.)

The Spontaneous Remonetization of Gold

The growing use of gold as a store of value to hedge against inflation must ultimately set the stage for a spontaneous remonetization of gold. As the number of people holding gold and seeking to acquire it as a form of savings increase, cases will arise where buyers who possess gold encounter sellers of consumption goods who want to acquire gold. In such cases, gold will be able to be exchanged directly against goods. (For smaller exchanges the same will apply to silver.)

As the number of such cases increases, and people begin to realize that gold can be used as a medium of exchange, the number of people willing to accept gold in exchange for their goods or services will further increase. People who themselves have no desire to hold gold will nevertheless become willing to accept it, because they will know that there is a significant number of others willing to accept it from them. Their willingness to accept gold will make still others willing to accept it. After a while, everyone will be willing to accept gold as a means of payment. At that point, gold will once again be money. (Indeed, this is precisely how gold became established as money in the first place. Its suitability for saving and its widespread use as a store of value gave rise to its use as a medium of exchange and then as a universally acceptable medium of exchange.)

Of course, the process of the spontaneous remonetization of gold could be aborted. The ownership of gold could simply be prohibited under threat of severe penalties. Or the process could be greatly slowed by various lesser restrictions, such as unfavorable treatment of gold transactions by the tax authorities and refusal of the courts to enforce gold contracts.

Such measures would not save the paper money system, though they might prolong its existence for a while. Their ultimate effect would be to convert the inflation-caused destruction of paper money into a destruction of money *per se*, for paper money would be destroyed and could not be replaced by anything else.

To find a historical parallel for such a catastrophe, one must go all the way back to the Roman Empire, which destroyed its coinage by a century of debasement, prohibited the private ownership and exchange of the precious metals, and was then left without the use of money. Rome's inflation and its prohibition of privately owned gold destroyed the Roman economy, whose extensive division of labor could not survive on a barter basis. The inflationist policy of the Roman government was thus responsible for the destruction of ancient civilization and the coming of feudalism—a primitive system of local self-sufficiency that did not depend on the use of money. Such would be the result of the destruction of money in modern times, as well.

Price Implications of Remonetizing Gold

The potential real value of gold—the potential buying power of the gold ounce—must be considered in the light of gold's potential reemergence as money.

If gold is to re-emerge as money through market processes, it will do so in an environment in which unbacked paper money in any form is thoroughly discredited. Thus gold would be likely to re-emerge as money under conditions in which it (along with silver in a subsidiary role) constituted the only form of money. This would not imply the total absence of paper and checkbook money — far from it — but only that all money that was not gold would have to be 100 percent backed by gold.

The present stock of money in the United States is roughly $400 billion. The present world stock of money can be estimated at roughly four times that, or $1.6 trillion.

If the world stock of money were to be comprised of gold, or in any way effectively limited by the quantity of gold, it would have a value equivalent to subtantially more than $1.6 trillion in present buying power. A gold money or one strictly limited by the quantity of gold, would be vastly more desirable to own than the present moneys of the world. And thus a unit of such money would have a substantially greater value. Thus, even though it may seem paradoxical, a world economy based on gold would possess a much larger money stock in terms of buying power than the present world economy.

To form some estimate of just how great the world's money stock might be in terms of buying power, one should realize that while today the U.S. money stock is less than one-sixth of U.S. GNP, in 1946 it was slightly more than one-half of GNP. A money stock of gold could well bear a similar ratio to GNP. On a world basis today, this would imply a money stock of $5 trillion — given an assumed world GNP of $10 trillion.

Taking the total world stock of gold, inclusive of all central bank holdings, at two billion ounces, the implied buying power of an ounce of gold would be $2,500 in 1980 purchasing power. Taking the world stock of gold at three billion ounces, the implied buying power of an ounce of gold would be $1,667 in 1980 purchasing power.

Silver's Role as Money

The potential buying power of gold under a 100 percent reserve system has important implications for the monetary role of silver. If an ounce of gold were to have a buying power in the neighborhood of $2,000, the smallest practical size gold coin — roughly equal to the old U.S. gold dollar or today's Mexican two peso gold piece — would have a buying power of about $100. This is far too large for the great majority of day-to-day retail transactions. If coins were to be used in such transactions, they would have to be made of something less valuable than gold.

This is where the monetary role of silver enters. Historically, silver was valued for centuries at approximately one-fifteenth the value of gold. If this ratio were to apply again (and it existed briefly in the early part of 1980), an ounce of silver would have a buying power of about $133. A silver dime, containing approximately 7/100 of an ounce of silver, would have a buying power of a little more than $9 of 1980 purchasing power.

Such a buying power of gold and silver, while extreme in comparison with what we are accustomed to today, is not extreme by historical standards. In fact, it enables us to understand the prices paid in earlier centuries. If, for example, we think of 7/100 of an ounce of silver as having a buying power of nine present dollars, it becomes understandable how menus from the mid-nineteenth century could offer a full meal for 5 cents — 5 cents was the silver equivalent of several of our present dollars. It also becomes clear how even the purchasing power of a penny was significant and why half-cent coins were necessary.

Of course, all of the figures we have given as estimates of potential buying power are nothing more than estimates. They could easily be off the mark by a substantial margin. They are significant only as rough approximations. If that is how they are interpreted, they will serve a useful purpose. For they provide a powerful indication of what to expect from inflation and why to expect it."

The Prospect of Hyperinflation

Even though supply and demand factors alone will cause a multiple long-term price rise in the precious metals (particularly silver and platinum), it is inflationary expectations that will be principally responsible for their price movements in the 1982-85 period. These are the expectations for progressively greater inflation in all currencies, not only in the United States dollar. What is not commonly understood yet by most of the general public is that under actual official policies *all* currencies are effectively pegged to the U.S. dollar and when it goes — they go.

Clearly evident upon a close examination of Chart 29 is the long-term effect of ongoing inflation of the money supply on the purchasing value of the dollar since 1950. As the chart shows, the dollar's purchasing power has been declining at an accelerating rate.

Also apparent, since 1960, is that the uptrend of money-supply inflation by all three measures inversely leads the downtrend rate of dollar depreciation, and that all of these trends are exponential.

Increases in the dollar money supply are based upon increases in U.S. federal debt through debt monetization by the Federal Reserve Bank. Thus, deficit spending (creating federal debt) is the root source of inflation. And the close long-term correlation between increases in federal debt outstanding and the Consumer Price Index (a measure of price inflation), is clear when viewing the two plotted together in Chart 30. These two also obviously form exponential curves leading to infinity and hyperinflation.

We have seen deficits (i.e., increases in federal debt) every year since 1969, and in most years they keep getting bigger because out-of-control government spending keeps rising at a faster clip than government's income. This is true again this year and will again be the case in 1983, 1984 and beyond, in spite of Mr. Reagan's best efforts to "balance the budget by 1984." Thus, because of uncontrollable and soaring federal spending, deficits and debt for this decade as a whole, one can be sure that inflation for the rest of the 1980s will be far worse than in the 1970s. 1982, like 1972, will be the springboard for a jump into new record rates of inflation in the following year and beyond. The minimum inflation outlook is persistent double-digit inflation, over 10 percent, with recurrent surges

Chart 29
U.S. Money Supply Versus Purchasing Power of the Dollar

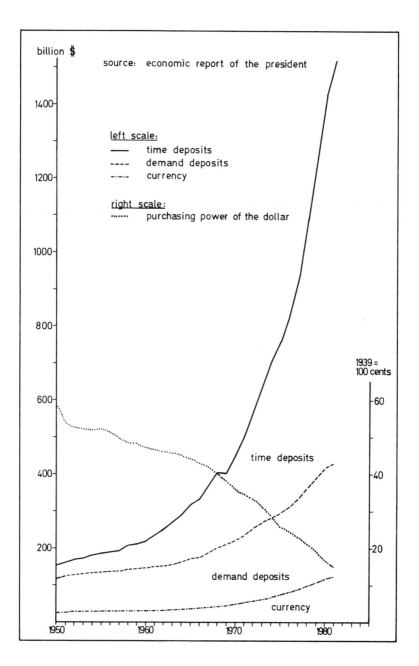

Chart 30
Gross Federal Debt Vs. Consumer Prices

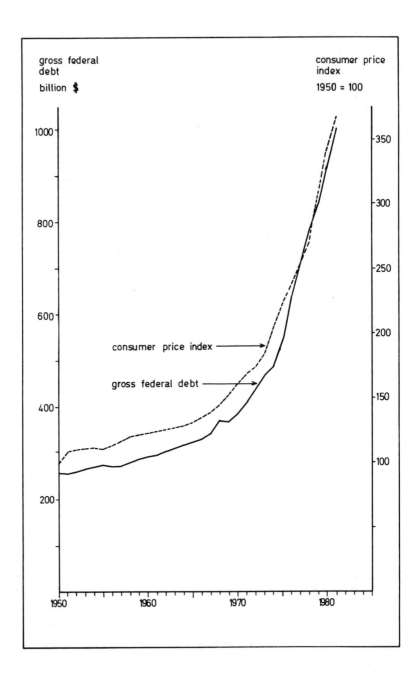

to the 20 to 30 percent range. The more likely outlook is that a surge to much higher double-digit rates, perhaps as early as 1985, will lead to triple-digit inflation, hyperinflation and effective destruction of national currencies, resulting in astronomic prices for the precious metals.

Under either outlook, the rate of inflation and precious-metals prices will wax and wane year-to-year while going much higher over multi-year periods.

As the trend toward hyperinflation develops in 1983 and beyond, prices of virtually everything will begin to soar in nominal dollar terms. With this prospect, any specific dollar price projection for the precious metals is quite meaningless. Because of hyperinflation silver might eventually be priced in thousands, millions, or billions of dollars per ounce. What does count is the confident outlook for a *real-value doubling or trebling as a minimum increase* (i.e., doubling or trebling in terms of gold within a few years). We could recite here all the other economic and monetary influences, including the histories of other hyperinflations and especially the German experience following World War I. A hyperinflationary scenario guarantees vastly higher prices for precious metals, especially silver, but that material has already been covered elsewhere.[2]

For the first time since the 1930s, the economies of the Western nations are all in very serious economic trouble at the same time, and for many of the same reasons. Any analogy with the 'thirties can easily be carried too far, however, leading to a wrong conclusion about what to expect on the deflation-bust versus inflation-bust question.

In the same way that double-digit (billions) budget deficits in the 'sixties brought double-digit inflation in the 'seventies, we can expect that triple-digit (billions) budget deficits early in the 'eighties will bring triple-digit inflation later in the 1980s. This is what we expect. We could be wrong; *it is possible that there could be a re-run of the 1930s* but we think that is highly unlikely. . .one chance in 10 at the most.

There are four significant differences in the economic mix today compared with the early 'thirties:
(1) The massive worldwide deflation and depression of the

---

[2]See *The Coming Currency Collapse — And What You Can Do About It* (1980: Books in Focus, 160 East 38th Street, #31B, New York, N.Y. 10016).

'thirties has been in the history and economics textbooks for a generation now. It teaches academics and officials the lesson that in the context of generally depressed business conditions *a central bank must act as prompt lender of last resort* to all distressed major banks (and their major debtors, including large corporations, nonbank financial institutions and even foreign nations under recent legislation), or face an uncontrollable deflationary spiral.

(2) The central banks and national treasuries of all Western nation-states today are under *none* of the constraints of a gold-based system. They are under no obligation to anyone—not even to each other—to redeem in specie, and also under no obligation even to maintain fixed exchange rates with others. One and all of them can "create" any amount of "money" at will, as necessary, to "save" (or not save) any near-bankrupt they choose—and as many as they choose.

(3) Today, communications, creation of fiat money credits and electronic transfers of those credits to wherever needed, are instantaneous. Thus the likelihood of any "accidental" deflation due to communications delays or lack of information is much less.

(4) Today, as contrasted to the 'thirties, we have a highly developed world market economy. At the mere cost of ink, a few phone calls and telexes, some nation-states (less badly-off) have selfish reasons to, and will, provide financial help to another in trouble (e.g., Britain currently).

The ultimate outcome, possible in only two or three years (perhaps longer), will be the complete destruction of paper currency values—which is the *only* way the massive debt accumulation of the last 40 years can be liquidated—that is, in effect, a cancellation of all debts. This is why we advise you to get rid of all dollar-denominated "investments" and acquire and hold things of real, tangible value—particularly the precious metals, and especially silver.

CHAPTER X

How, How Much, Where and When to Invest in Precious Metals

There are four basic ways one can invest in precious metals:

(1) Buy stocks of a mining company;
(2) Buy a futures contract;
(3) Buy United States, Canadian, Mexican or other silver coins in bulk, buy low-premium privately minted silver or gold coins[1] or buy Krugerrands or other low-premium gold coins;
(4) Buy silver or gold bullion, or platinum bars. Another relatively new and less direct way, pertaining only to silver, is to invest in silverbacked bonds.

As you would expect, there are peculiar advantages and disadvantages to each of the above methods. The most direct and least expensive way to profit from higher precious-metals prices of course, is to buy bullion (the metal itself) in commercial grade bars. But let's consider each method in turn.

Mining Stocks

Silver, gold and platinum mining stocks are available on United States and Canadian stock exchanges and on many other exchanges throughout the world. Individuals acting through member brokers can buy such mining stocks in these markets at prices ranging upward of a few cents per share.

---

[1]The largest private minter of low-priced gold and silver coins is Gold Standard Corporation, 1127-1131 West 41st Street, Kansas City, Missouri 64111.

There is a problem with mining company shares that does not exist in owning the metal itself. The problem is the same as with stocks in any other industry—selection. There are hundreds of mining companies from which to choose. When one chooses and buys shares in a given company, part of the risk is the uncertainty of whether that particular management will succeed in making operating profits and be able to pay dividends. The great majority of them fail to do so, and this is likely to get worse as their costs are forced ever higher by bureaucratic over-regulation (particularly in the area of environmental pollution controls). Further, mining companies generally now carry long-term debt burdens at high interest rates, and most mining company managers in this respect and in other ways are not better able to cope with the profit-destroying effects of roller-coasting runaway inflation than are the managers of other types of businesses.

Further, most silver is not produced by silver mining companies as such, but by copper, lead and zinc mining companies (which produce silver as a by-product). Consequently, these companies will not necessarily profit from increased silver prices.

For maximum leverage, only stocks of mines whose *principal output is precious metal* should be purchased. A good stock broker will be able to guide an investor in selecting some of these. However, one should be careful because there are relatively few such companies (and few knowledgeable brokers[2]).

Futures Contracts

On the Commodity Exchange, Inc. (in New York), or on the Chicago Board of Trade, an individual acting through a commodities broker can buy contracts to accept delivery of silver, gold or platinum a few or many months into the future. Since few traders actually take delivery, these markets are frequently referred to as "paper markets."

---

[2]One good broker we can recommend who specializes in such stocks is Mr. Sam Parks, 240-500 Union Street, Seattle, Washington 98101. Phone (206) 624-9026 or (800) 426-0598.

In light of the markets' activity during 1979-80 (as detailed in Chapter II), readers may be disinclined to invest in futures; and there are other sound reasons why these markets should be avoided by the average investor.

Futures markets are a way of speculating in short-term price movements — not of investing in precious metals. Prices for future delivery are more volatile than bullion prices, the most distant months being the most volatile. *This is a market for full-time professional traders and floor brokers seeking short-term trading profits.*

Usually, even those who put up substantially more than the minimum required margin and who intend to hold their position "long-term" (one to two years), soon find themselves adding to their position (on thinner margin). They then find themselves succumbing to the temptation to trade in and out, seeking short-term profits but losing their capital instead.

It is not possible to make a long-term precious metals investment in the futures markets. All futures contracts have an expiration date beyond which you cannot hold the contract. When your contract comes up for delivery, you must — repeat, *must* — either sell or take delivery. Selling can either produce an unwanted capital loss, or more likely, a capital gain which you may or may not wish to realize at that time. You can only avoid the inconvenient capital gain by paying in full and taking delivery if you have enough cash (or by pledging your precious metal as collateral and financing the purchase).

Further, when this is done, the record of the metal stored in the registered exchange warehouse is simply changed to reflect your ownership. Your investment has thus become a sitting duck for government seizure, later when the money system breaks down — or sooner, at the government's convenience.

To escape this threat you have two realistic choices. You can either sell at the first hint that government confiscation is being or might be considered, perhaps thus being forced to take the taxable gain or loss you may have wanted to delay or avoid; or you can ship your precious metal at great effort and expense to a reliable Swiss bank (or other safe haven) for storage. How much simpler if you had purchased through a Swiss bank in the first place.

In view of the foregoing, if you are already involved in trading futures you should, in our opinion, sell out and begin all over by buying silver outright.

Silver Coins

United States silver dollars, half-dollars, quarters and dimes minted prior to 1965 have a silver content of 90 percent.

Bulk U.S. silver coins are a unique investment. They have the same appreciation potential as bullion because of their metal content. In addition they offer three basic advantages:

(1) They have an absolute floor value—their spending value as money. They can always be spent for at least a portion of their cost, no matter what happens in the silver markets. They are both real money *and* a vehicle for capital preservation and gain.

(2) Over very long time periods, they have the potential to appreciate more in value than bullion. Coins can always be converted into bullion, but bullion cannot legally be made into coins.

(3) In the event of a complete currency collapse, U.S. silver coinage will reappear as a standard medium of exchange in private markets, at a high multiple of its face value.

In spite of these advantages, we do not recommend U.S. silver coins as an investment for substantial amounts if they are to be held within the territorial jurisdiction of the United States. We do recommend that each individual (or family) purchase one or two ($1,000 face-amount) bags of silver coins from a reputable domestic coin dealer. Pay for them in full, take delivery, and keep them in your own possession as an emergency reserve fund of real spending money which will always buy food and other necessities, at any time, and under virtually any circumstances.

Each bag of $1,000 face-amount of U.S. silver coins weighs about 720 troy ounces. Through most of the 1970s and in 1980, these coins traded for slightly less than their metal content, usually approximately reflecting the melting and refining costs to convert them into bullion. However, $1,000 face-amount bags of silver coins were recently (August 1981) selling for $8,545.00 with the Spot New York silver price at $8.82, a premium of 35 percent over their bullion content. If this premium continues, as we expect, it effectively precludes any further coin-melting. The disappearance during 1981 of this formerly substantial flow of silver into the markets is one of the reasons we are very bullish in our 1983-85 outlook for silver.

An alternative, with less risk of volatility due to changes in the premium up or down, is low-premium, privately minted silver (or gold) coins. Presently, there is only one large private minter of such low-priced coins (see footnote 1). However growing demand for such coins will no doubt spur both competition and widespread availability of these coins in coming years.

Beyond the recommended "insurance" investment in U.S. 90 percent silver coins, or an equal amount of privately minted silver coins, held in one's own possession, we recommend 40 percent to 50 percent of one's financial capital be invested in silver bullion purchased through a Swiss bank.

Silver Bullion

Purchasing silver bullion can be done quite as easily as dealing with a domestic broker. One can write to a Swiss bank directly and ask for account-opening forms and information on silver bullion purchases.

In 1967, to simplify such investments overseas, I devised a carefully constructed program for buying precious metals through a reliable Swiss bank. This program, which has made many millions for those who have followed it, is administered by:

Economic Research Counselors,
585 16th Street, Suite 212,
West Vancouver, B.C.,
Canada V7V 4S2

You may contact ERC by letter or telephone[3] for complete details — no obligation, of course. As of this writing, the minimum rquired to open an account at the Swiss bank

---

[3]You can call *toll-free* by dialing (800) 426-5270 (from Alaska, Hawaii and Washington State call *collect* (206) 332-5159; in Canada call *collect* (604) 926-5476).

handling ERC clients is U.S. $10,000.

Ownership of silver bullion is the most direct, lowest-risk, and least expensive way to profit from the expected long-term price advance in silver. When purchases are made for cash, silver bullion is a safer and more conservative investment than any paper security — because the buyer owns the metal itself, a precious metal that can never lose all of its value, as any paper security could.

Margin purchases are recommended only to those who want the enhanced potential of a leveraged purchase and who understand the use of margin.

Buying bullion directly through a Swiss bank gives you several advantages. First, there is no expiration date on fully paid (or margined) spot precious-metal positions with a Swiss bank. You pick your own time to buy or sell and accept profits or losses. In addition, you can sell any portion whenever you wish, taking incremental profits or losses in years when they bring you the greatest tax advantage.

A further advantage is that, theoretically at least, you need *never* sell and pay capital gains tax. Instead you can borrow against your holding (a non-taxable transaction) and later pass the metal and the loan on to your heirs so that *you* never have to pay a tax on any gain. And, your interest payments are tax deductible!

Finally, unlike U.S. futures contracts, you can borrow against your metal and have such loans denominated in any one of most major currencies. This will enable you to take advantage of declining relative currency values and/or international interest-rate differentials.[4]

A Super-Safe Silver Investment

In 1980 the Sunshine Mining Company issued silver-backed bonds that offer both an interest return and a silver-redemption feature.

---

[4]ERC investment clients, under the guidance of Economic Research Counselors, are informed about which of the major currencies are the most advisable to owe at differing times, depending on interest rates and the exchange-rate outlook.

These bonds represent a near-perfect hedged silver investment.

The Sunshine Mine, in the rich Coeur d'Alene Mining District of northern Idaho, is the largest single American mine primarily engaged in the production of silver. But Sunshine Mining Company also owns silver mines in Nevada, including two-thirds of the picturesquely named "Sixteen-to-One" (after the historic ratio between the prices of silver and gold).

In April 1980 they put on the market (through Drexel, Burnham, Lambert) $25 million worth of $1,000 face-value bonds, redeemable at the holder's option at maturity for either dollars or 50 ounces of silver. A similar $25-million issue followed in December 1980. They are due on April 15, 1995. The coupon, or interest rate, is 8½ percent (in dollars, not tied to silver). If after April 15, 1985 the silver price for 50 ounces is more than twice the dollar face-value of the bonds for at least 30 consecutive days, Sunshine reserves the right to redeem the bonds. Whenever they do redeem them, they pledge to pay bondholders either $1,000 in cash (the par value) or the then market value of 50 ounces of silver, *whichever is greater.*

This is especially attractive if one can buy these bonds at a discount from par value, which is the case as this is written. With 100 equalling the $1,000 par value, the price of the bonds near the silver price peak in 1980 was as high as 145. At this writing they are at record lows, hovering around 85 (or $850 per $1,000 par value) for December's issue, and 88 for the April issue with current yields of, respectively, 10 percent and 9.6 percent. The ideal time to buy these bonds, of course, would be when interest rates are peaking and silver prices are bottoming together. It's not going to happen that way, so the best the investor can do is to spread his purchases over a period of time. However, if it appears rather likely that either the silver-price low or the interest-rate peak is past (as we expect both will be sometime in 1982), then one should buy immediately. We don't think interest rates will get much higher than the late 1981 highs, nor silver much lower than, say $8 (even though it may stay depressed for months well into 1982). But at any price under par for this $1,000 face-value guarantee, regardless of what silver does in 1982, we believe these bonds are cheap enough to recommend that everyone buy at least one.[5]

There are also tax advantages for Americans to these asset bonds which straight dollar fixed-income instruments lack. While the bond's interest is taxed at normal rates, any rise of the asset value—in this case silver—above the bond's face value would be treated as a capital gain, taxable at 28 percent.

Gold and Platinum

After silver coins and silver bullion, another 10 to 15 percent of available investment funds should go into gold coins. The Krugerrand is our preferred choice among official coins because of its low premium and high liquidity. These can be bought and held in possession (if one has secure storage) or can be purchased through a Swiss bank and held by the bank. Or both arrangements may be utilized, for different portions of one's total holdings. (One can select privately minted gold coins for the portion to be held in possession.)

For larger portfolios (over $50,000), another 10 to 15 percent should go into gold bullion purchased through and held by a Swiss bank. A further 5 to 10 percent should be put into platinum. Cash credit balances should comprise no more than 10 to 15 percent of one's investment portfolio. These should be carried in a Swiss franc deposit (savings) account or, for very large sums, Swiss-franc-denominated certificates of deposit.

(For a thorough discussion of the merits of investing in Switzerland and the pre-eminence of the Swiss franc among national currencies in the 1982-85 period, see Appendix C.)

When to Buy

Most investors will not trust their own minds. They are incapable of buying unless they can see a bandwagon already in

[5]They are traded on the New York Bond Exchange and the *Wall Street Journal* lists them daily, as do most good metropolitan newspapers' financial sections. The December 1980 issue is marked SunsS; the April one, Sunsh.

progress. Consequently, they always buy after most of the price movement has taken place.

The nature of the marketplace dictates that the man who will make the largest profit must be the man who will buy and hold when no one else can see what he sees. He buys because he knows what must inevitably come — even if no one else agrees with him at that time. Consequently, he buys before the stampede — and makes the largest profit. He doesn't act on tips, guesses or hunches. He sees a fundamental supply/demand discrepancy, acts upon what he sees, and then sits and waits for the inevitable. He is always in "too soon" — and he always makes far more than the man who later jumps on the bandwagon.

When should you buy precious metals or add to your present holdings? Right now! With present conditions and those we expect in 1982, you may be as much as six months too early or there may be a temporary adverse price fluctuation before the stampede begins. If either of these possibilities occurs, what will you have lost? But if you wait until you can see the bandwagon already in progress, you may wind up buying at a price 50 percent higher and you will have saved practically nothing in costs by waiting.

One Word of Caution

If, as you read this, silver is well over $20 an ounce and has doubled in a year or less, be careful. Under such circumstances you will probably be better off to wait a few months looking for a 25 to 30 percent decline. Or, if you do not want to wait, for fear that it might double again before there is any decline, then divide the dollar amount of your intended total purchase by ten and buy that fixed-dollar amount once each month over a ten-month period. This is called dollar-cost-averaging and it will achieve a lower average cost in volatile markets than you are likely to obtain in any other way.

A Final Note

Virtually everything said in this book is aimed at investors with liquid capital of from $10,000 to $100,000 to invest. We have limited the discussion to the handful of investments that we believe will best preserve capital value and offer the highest appreciation, with as much diversification as we think appropriate for the small to moderate investor in the 1980s.

For investment portfolios of six- or seven-digit proportions, we would recommend additional investments and more diversification in the years ahead. We would also recommend some form of professional management, depending on the size of the portfolio and the individual needs, desires and objectives of the investor.

One such management company we can recommend, with which we are connected in an advisory capacity, is Applied Austrian Advisers, Ltd., P.O. Box 472, Grand Cayman, British West Indies. AAA is an investment advisory company offering discretionary account management in worldwide securities, commodities and precious metals.

Alternatively, investors holding six- or seven-digit portfolios who want direct personal advice from the authors may write to:

Jerome F. Smith
Research Economist
Apartado 788, Centro Colon
San Jose, Costa Rica

Appendices

The Long History of Silver Money*

In the opinion of those who write on the subject, the first metals to be discovered and used by early man were gold, copper, and silver, in that order. In those days all three must have been much more abundant and obvious than they are now, the readily accessible deposits having long since been assiduously collected. . . . The metallurgical laboratories of Stone Age man were in the ashes of his domestic fires and, still more, in the paths of forest fires caused by the sun and by lightning. . . .

Just as the discoverers had associated the yellow color of gold with the sun, so they related the brilliant white of silver to the moon and no doubt called it by the appropriate name in their language while giving it the crescent symbol. . . .

Early History

. . . In the early period after its discovery, its attractions must have been very strong and interest rapid in growth so that, it seems, the forest fires became less accidental. The historian Diodorus Siculus, who wrote in Greek in the last

---

*Excerpted with permission from "The History of Silver" by Donald McDonald, Chapter 1 of *Silver — Economics, Metallurgy, and Use*, edited by Allison Butts, with Charles D. Coxe (D. Van Nostrand Co., Inc., Princeton, New Jersey).

century B.C., states (*Historical Library*, Book V, Chapter 2): "These places being covered with woods, it is said that in ancient times these mountains (the Pyrenees) were set on fire by shepherds and continued burning for many days and parched the earth so that an abundance of silver ore was melted and the metal flowed in streams of pure silver like a river." This picture will be quite familiar to anyone who has watched the discharge of a large cupel furnace.

So it comes about that in many of the earliest traditional records that we have, as well as in the evidence of graves and buried hoards, man in Southern Europe and the Near and Middle East is found to have been endowed with silver ornament and even to have used the metal in bulk as a token of wealth exchangable for goods, services, or ownership. By then these uses were established and it is clear that, although gold was still the monopoly of kings and priests, silver was the currency of the merchants in their trade and was used by weight for that purpose. Obviously, then, for a very long time, man in those regions had been locating and working larger deposits, no doubt mostly of galena, found in and around the areas of gathering civilizations.

As far as we know, the earliest work of any appreciable size was conducted by the predecessors of the Hittites in Cappadocia, in the eastern part of Asia Minor, apparently at some time in the fourth millenium B.C. There are records of a high state of civilization in this region in the third millenium, and jewelry and metal work were in full use. By B.C. 2000 or soon after, according to certain Cappadocian tablets dating from that time, not only were quantities of silver being exported to Assyria but there was a resident colony of Mesopotamian merchants in Cappadocia to forward this trade. From all this it is quite evident that, in these regions, the forest-fire period of production was well past by the fourth millenium B.C. and had been replaced by serious mining operations, at first probably of an open-cast nature but followed by underground work. This must have been accompanied by smelting work in furnaces with controlled cupellation to produce the pure metal required by the trade described above.

. . . about B.C. 500 the important Laurium silver-lead mines in Greece were opened. These are said to have been the mainstay of Athens for three centuries and its chief support in the Persian wars. They lasted until the 1st century A.D., and were then shut down. By that time silver, and even more so gold, was being eagerly sought by the nations for its high economic value, and mines were being exploited under the cruelest conditions of slavery by native peoples, by convicted criminals and even, in the next case, by black slaves imported from Africa. This was in the Spanish silver-lead mines, developed first by the Carthaginians and continued on a relatively large scale by the Romans after their victory in the Punic Wars.

Meanwhile an important new demand was growing up from India, in payment for what came to be called the Spice Trade. This traveled from Ceylon and the Malabar Coast of India to the Red Sea, across the sands of Egypt to the Nile and down to Alexandria, where, after the Egyptians had taken their share of the trade, it was picked up and distributed, first by the Phoenicians, then by the Carthaginians and later by the Romans. The spices, and with them the silks, fine cottons, ivories, and jade, served the luxury, first of Carthage and then of Imperial Rome. Fastidious tastes combined with the difficulties of storing food, especially through the winter, stimulated trade and silver flowed to India from the Spanish mines to pay for it. The fall of Western Rome (A.D. 476) and the Arab conquests put an end to the trade until Venice was in the position to restore it about 1200. From then it flourished until the Turks captured Constantinople in 1453. This, coupled with Vasco da Gama's discovery of the Cape route to the East, put both the Spice Trade and the silver that paid for it on the seas, where both have continued ever since.

In the 8th century the Moorish invasion stopped the Spanish mining and there followed in Europe from then to the 15th century a disturbed period, in the course of which a certain amount of silver became available from Bohemia and Transylvania, but most of the supplies were obtained not from the earth but from a redistribution by means of war and plunder.

Fortunately, in time for the great developments in world trade in the 16th and 17th centuries, and possibly in part a cause of them, came the Spanish discoveries after 1520 of silver in their new Empire in Central and South America, chiefly in Mexico, Bolivia, and Peru. Not only were these enormously larger than all earlier finds, but the ore was much richer in silver . . .

In the first half of the 17th century Europe also obtained large quantities of silver from Japan. At first this trade was exploited by the Portuguese, but they made themselves unpopular and were expelled in 1624, being replaced by the Dutch, who continued the business into the 19th century.

Apart from this, Spanish America supplied the world with silver until the colonies there revolted in 1800-1820 and export was disturbed. This caused much difficulty from the monetary point of view, but the existence of large stocks, the greater use of gold, and the evolution of banking systems staved off crisis until the situation was relieved by the discovery of great new silver resources in the Sierra Nevada in the United States. These soon established the United States as the largest producer (a position it retained until about 1900) and, although this caused a crop of problems of its own, there was no longer any world shortage of silver; as time went on, too, an increasing proportion of that metal began to appear as a by-product in the production of the principal nonferrous industrial metals, copper, lead, and zinc, most of the ores of which contained some silver.

Silver for Use

The factors determining the uses to which silver was put by early man were first its beautiful white color; second its resistance to corrosion, which allowed it to be buried in the earth for long periods without deterioration; and third its relative and maintained scarcity. These created a demand for it both as ornamentation and as a store of wealth, and brought about its eventual distribution far and wide.

. . . fine silver produced by all these processes is a relatively soft metal and, in the course of use, wears away. To avoid this, from very early days it has been alloyed by silversmiths with a small quantity of copper, normally not more than 10 percent. The most famous of these alloys is probably the English sterling (silver 925 parts per thousand, copper 75) which was formulated about A.D. 1200 and is employed for jewelry and plate, as well as formerly for coinage. . . .

For a century or two past, silver has been used for the embellishment of cheaper and stronger metals. The principal means for effecting this are: (1) by covering with thin sheet ("cladding"), (2) by electrochemical deposition in elec-troplating, and (3) by chemical deposition as in mirrors. The earliest form of cladding with silver was probably "close plating," in which thin silver foil was pressed onto the heated base metal (usually iron) covered with a thin film of tin. A pass or two with a soldering-iron would melt the tin and form a joint. An advance from this was the English "Sheffield Plate" of between 1750 and 1850. Here a slab of silver, bound by wire to a thicker block of copper, was placed in a heated furnace. Melting took place at the joint at a temperature well below the melting points of both metals (at or near the eutec-tic point) and, after cooling, there was a perfect joint and the block of "bi-metal" could be rolled down to any dimensions required. Considerable artistic ability was applied to this material over the century of its vogue and the product is still valued by collectors.

In due course, however, Sheffield Plate was displaced by a cheaper product produced by electroplating. It had been known for many years that silver could be deposited from solu-tions of its salts upon some other metals simply by immersing them and the process of "water silvering" was practiced in a small way. It was also appreciated that this technique was much improved if the deposition took place in an electrolytic cell. However, this idea did not become interesting until the invention of useful electrical batteries, and even then it required the introduction of the dynamo in the 1870s and 1880s to make it a definite commercial success. . . .

The cleanliness of silver and its resistance to the acids of food, cooking, and digestion no doubt drew man's attention early to the fact that silver can be inserted into the human body and left there for long periods without any ill effects. The use of thin silver plates after trephining of the skull, of silver wires to prevent the movement of broken bones, and of drainage tubes has been practiced by surgeons for many centuries and there is no doubt that in establishing the suitability of the metal for these purposes, its now well-known bactericidal properties were unconsciously realized. Another use for silver was in dentistry, where an amalgam of a silver-tin alloy with mercury can be molded at the temperature of the mouth, after which it quickly hardens to a polishable finish.

At about the time that silver was first being utilized in the kitchen and dining room and possibly even earlier, it could be seen in the dressing-room and boudoir, where boxes for powders and unguents go back to the early civilizations. Silver was used for all kinds of pins, brooches, and fasteners, for boxes and bottle tops, for scent-sprays, and even for chamber-pots and bidets until a height of luxury was reached in the French court of the mid-18th century that had never been achieved before and never since. One of the earliest articles on the toilet table was, of course, the mirror, at first a plain polished plate or disk of silver. This lasted until early in the 14th century, when there emerged from Venice a better reflecting surface produced by laying an amalgam of tin and mercury on glass. The world used this until 1855 when a young Frenchman named Petitjean, following up a fundamental discovery by the great German chemist Liebeg some twenty years before, found it possible to reduce a solution of silver nitrate by means of tartaric acid and tartrates to a real and permanent mirror-film of metallic silver, again on glass. . . .

We can now leave the domestic uses of silver and consider the technical ones. The first of these arises from the fact that it is the best conductor of electricity of all the metals and this, coupled with its notable resistance to heat and corrosion, opens up for its use a wide field in electricity and electronics and in the engineering connected with both. This of course has come about primarily in the present century. Previously silver had been largely monopolized by those who dealt in finance and money and there was relatively little left for anyone else. On the other hand, electrical engineering had not developed to the point at which the properties of silver were essential to it; it was still able to make full and satisfactory use of copper. This industry could afford to continue to leave silver to the moneyers. Another property of silver used in those days was its power, when mixed in certain proportions with other metals, to make very sound joints between metal parts. Silver solders, as they were called, were being made, but only in small quantities — enough to enable silversmiths to stick their pieces together and to attach feet onto pots. Not until later did the practice of silver brazing arise. Silver also to some extent possesses catalytic properties and has come into use quite extensively in the vapor-phase oxidation of a number of organic compounds. Finally, there is photography with all its variants, such as cinematography, metallography, micro-photography, radiography, spectrography, etc. For all these silver is as the life-blood — not as metal but as its salt, silver bromide — upon the action of light on which the whole photo-graphic process depends. Light, to a degree depending on its intensity, disturbs the structure of this compound and renders it selectively reducible to metallic silver by certain special chemical reducing agents known as "developers." This yields a negative picture which can be readily converted into a positive one by repeating the process under different conditions.

The Monetary Uses

From the early days of its availablility until the threshold of our own times the largest use of silver has been the monetary one, as a safe store of value and as a means of its exchange. And it is remarkable that even at the very dawn of history there appear to be plentiful supplies of it moving about Europe, North Africa, and Asia in the course of trade. The historians who lived in the last millenium B.C., especially Herodotus, Polybius, and the authors of the Biblical Pentateuch, make many references to it, the best known of which is that of Abraham's purchase of the grave of Macphelah in Genesis 23, for which he paid "four hundred shekels of silver, current money with the merchant," at a date probably somewhere between B.C. 2000 and 1500. There was also, of course, the ever-growing quantity of silver that flowed east to finance the Spice Trade, fostered by the Phoenicians in the second millenium B.C. One wonders where all the silver came from and can only surmise that it happened in the ways and places mentioned above, reinforced of course by raiding, theft, and war.

The original form in which silver entered trade was in actual "pieces of silver," consisting of roughly melted ingots or lumps of cut or sawn metal. The value was fixed by weight and all the ancient units of value were weights. The Phoenician unit, based on Babylonian usage, was the talent (about 1500 troy ounces) and the Hebrew unit the shekel (about half an ounce, with later a heavier one twice that weight); in due course other such units were the original English pound, the Indian tola, and the Chinese tael.

From such beginnings evolved coins. First, the original "piece" had to be stamped with marks indicating weight and fineness. . . .the irregularity of the shapes of the "pieces" made them difficult to count, so gradually the trading world came to coins that could be piled one on the other. Herodotus thought that the Lydians were the first people to use primitive coins of both gold and silver in the shape of a bean, and certainly Croesus, the last king of Lydia (B.C. 568-554) used both metals as coinage in a fixed ratio of value. Greek coins soon followed and after that the spread was rapid throughout the Mediterranean area, although there seem to have been none in Egypt, Assyria, Babylonia, or Phoenicia, business there still being carried out by weight.

The demand for coins and the continual growth of the trade with India made great claims on the supplies of silver. The

Greek mines had supported Athens in its great days, but they were exhausted by the first century A.D. By then, however, the Carthaginians had exploited the mines in Spain between B.C. 480 and 206, when Rome, after the Punic Wars, took them over together with the trade with India which they financed. In B.C. 269 Rome had formally adopted silver as part of her monetary system and introduced the silver *denarius* (4.73 g of fine silver), which in B.C. 207 became full legal tender. All this put further burdens on the Spanish mines, where conditions of slavery and forced labor were maintained until the Arab conquest in the 8th century put an end to that source of supply.

The coins were now establishing themselves in three classes: gold for governments and the wealthy, silver for merchants and their trade, and copper, brass, or bronze for the day-to-day needs of ordinary people. It has already been mentioned that Croesus, King of Lydia, coined his gold and silver in a fixed value ratio, and this idea was continued. It was important that it should. With gold coins the nominal and intrinsic values were normally (in the absence of debasement or clipping) the same, but with silver the nominal value was usually considerably more than the intrinsic, a state of affairs which reaches its peak with paper money. Any overproduction of these soon begins to depreciate the real value of the currency in question and to inflate the local prices for goods.

The gold-silver ratio therefore provided a means for checking an excess of silver coin and restraining inflation. Soon after Rome started coining, the ratio settled down in the neighborhood of 1 (for gold): 10 (for silver), and it is a most astonishing thing that, with all the fluctuations in supply and world trade, it was still 1:11 in 1492; even by 1760 it had only moved to 1:14, and by 1860 to 1:15. Much has been written about this ratio and the factors that caused temporary and local movements in it, but yet on the whole kept it so relatively stable for so long a time. Here there is space only for a crude oversimplification which says that the ratio moved, or did not move, according to the balance of the availability of supplies of the two metals and the volume of trade that was seeking to use them; and there are those who have believed that each of these factors could act upon the other. Whatever the truth of that may be, it is quite evident that, toward the end of the 19th century, great disturbances occurred on both sides of the balance; these will be discussed below.

At the peak of the power of Rome in, say, the second century A.D., the main flow of silver along the arteries of world trade could be placed on either side of a line drawn on a modern map from Gibraltar to Alexandria and then to Colombo and on to Manila. Silver moved eastward and in return back came the spices, the silks, and the cottons that were so important to the luxurious civilizations of Carthage, Rome, and, later, Venice. No doubt some of the silver still moved in pieces and bars, but more and more coinage took over the currency duty.

The early coins were nearly all small, as befitted a subsidiary coinage, but they were an inconvenience in international trade and a demand began to arise for a larger standard coin. The response came from the mines in Central Europe in the Erz Gebirge, which had become the principal silver supplier to Europe in the period between the end of the Western Roman Empire and the Spanish conquest of Mexico. At Joachimsthal on the Bohemian side there was so much silver that in 1486 a local mint was set up to produce the first large trade coins. Naturally they were first called Joachimsthalers, quickly shortened to thalers, then to daler and, as soon as they reached the area of the *lingua franca* of the sea, dollars.

By that time the Spaniards were minting the silver that they had discovered in Mexico and spreading the product all over the coast of the Atlantic and Pacific oceans. The unit of their currency and the fundamental silver coin was the *real* (3.54 g of fine silver); they also had a trading coin, the Piece of Eight *(reales)*. A demand for this latter coin which was practically worldwide brought about huge mintings of it, not only at home in Spain but also, from about 1540, in Mexico. Thus soon it was Spanish "dollars," as they were everywhere known, that dominated the world's maritime trade. They appeared in the 18th century in two forms, the Pillar Dollar and the Carolus Dollar. The latter bore the head of King Charles

IV of Spain, and the former derived its name from the appearance on its reverse of the Royal Arms of Spain, of which the supporters are not the usual heraldic beasts but two baroque architectural columns, said to represent the Pillars of Hercules at Gibraltar, around which wreathed a wide ribbon with a Latin inscription. Soon, with increasing pressure of business, the bookkeepers of the time had to find a symbol to indicate this currency in their accounts, and someone arrived at a suitable one consisting of two upright lines to represent the two pillars and an S-twirl for the wreathed ribbon, giving the world the dollar-sign that it has used ever since. The Spanish dollar of course continued to be the normal currency in the Americas and in 1796, because of the familiarity of the public with it, it was used as the basis of the currency of the new Republic of the United States of America.

The discovery of the silver resources of the Americas and the minting there of Spanish coins led to the establishment of trade with the Spice Islands of Asia precisely similar to that of the Carthaginians and Romans eastward from the Mediterranean. Between 1565 and 1815 the Manila Galleon passed regularly, sometimes once a year, sometimes more often, from Acapulco to Manila and back, carrying the familiar silks, cottons, jade, ivories, and spices one way, and silver in Spanish Dollars, minted in Mexico, the other. And when the Spanish-American Revolution came and Mexico obtained its independence, the trade continued and, after about 1850, the Mexican dollar in its turn became the principal currency of the Yangtze valley and the China ports. These coins, like their predecessors, were used by the Chinese people in their normal trade, with brass "cash" for the small transactions. Large business was done in "sycee," ingots of silver shaped like their women's shoes but which to Western eyes looked more like boats. The weights of these varied up to 50 oz. and were recorded in taels, which also varied in different districts from 34 to 37 g of fine silver each.

Meanwhile, for some time in the Western world, change had been in the air. In 1747 Portugal, which had been receiving continually increasing quantities of gold from its Brazilian Empire, entirely demonetized silver and set up a single gold standard. Other countries followed, of which England in 1816, with her world-wide commercial connections, was the most important. The idea spread and by 1916 there were only a very few countries left in which silver was recognized as a standard, the most important of them of course being China.

The process was very much helped by the enormous yield of the new discoveries of silver in the United States from the 1860s, followed by others in Canada and Australia, which produced some repercussions in Europe. In 1865 several European states (France, Belgium, Switzerland, Italy, and later Greece) came together as the Latin Union and agreed to take action to maintain the ratio between gold and silver coined at 1:15½, by absorbing any excess of silver left at any time on the market. But this met with difficulties, the first coming from the newly unified Germany. A huge indemnity extracted from France at the end of the Franco-Prussian war enabled the new union to reorganize its formerly fragmented currency system and to demonetize silver in 1873, and after this, one by one, the nations slipped away to the gold standard.

The United States, with its large vested interest in silver, tried valiantly to stem the tide by agreeing to coin a large number of dollars each year, between 2 and 4 million under the Brand Act of 1878 and then three times as many under the Sherman Act of 1890. A very large accumulation of coin resulted and the Act had to be repealed in 1891. The surplus silver then inevitably poured into India and China. Rapid inflation in the former caused in 1893 the closing of the mints to free coinage. The Latin Union continued to trail along until World War I came with its inflations and restrictions of the movement of money, and these finally put an end to bimetalism as a practical policy. . . .

In 1920 a temporary rise in price forced several countries, including Britain and her sterling, to reduce the silver content of their coins from about 90 percent to 50 percent, a movement which reached its logical conclusion in 1946 when "sterling" ceased to use silver at all, an example followed by other nations in the years that followed.

After World War I there was also a general movement away from silver for money. The coinages of the vanished regimes (Russia, Austria), the reorganized regimes (France, Belgium, Norway, Germany, Italy, Spain), and the war-inflated nations like India poured out into the melting pot. Last of all, China disgorged some 7500 tons of silver coin in the mid-1930s. The price of silver on the London market fell and fell until in February, 1931, it touched the bottom at 12d per troy standard ounce. . . .

A Century of Government Intervention in Silver—A Chronology

1870s—Prior to this time, for many decades, most of the nations of the world freely coined silver presented at their mints. Thus the price in the U.S. for most of the 19th century was at the coinage value ($1.29) per troy ounce, or slightly above. However, following the worldwide currency depreciations and inflation accompanying the American Civil War, concurrent European conflicts and the rise of Bismarckian Welfare Statism, nearly all of the major nations suspended free coinage of silver. Germany was first (1871), then Sweden, Norway and Denmark (1872), the Netherlands and the United States (1873) ("The Crime of '73"), France and Belgium (1876), and finally Italy, Austria-Hungary, Russia and Switzerland (1878), ending free coinage of silver at any mint in Europe. Then began a long series of U.S. government subsidies and controls of domestic silver. Silver, having lost its "market" (while production was increasing), depreciated in price from $1.27/troy ounce in 1874 to $1.11 in 1880.

1878—Passage of the Bland-Allison Silver Purchase Act reintroduced the silver standard in the United States, and directed the U.S. Treasury to purchase $4 million in domestic silver per month, to be coined into silver dollars.

1879—Suspension of silver sales by German government. Marked diminution in production of California mines. U.S.

resumes specie payments (abandoned during Civil War green-back inflation, when all silver coins were privately withheld from circulation).

1881 — Conference in Paris respecting bi-metallism, adjourned without coming to any practical conclusion.

1882 — H.A. Hones writes *The Silver King.*

1883 — Introduction of cyanide process for extracting gold and silver.

1888 — Silver drops to new low of 92 cents in spite of massive Treasury purchases.

1889 — Coinage of silver unusually large.

1890 — U.S. flooded with silver dollars by now. Passage of Sherman Silver Purchase Act, replacing Bland-Allison Act, directs the Treasury to purchase $4.5 million in silver per month, to be paid for with a "new Treasury note."

1892 — Further depression in silver prices.

1893 — Indian mints closed to free coinage of silver. Under Grover Cleveland, Congress repeals Sherman Act on compulsory silver purchase. On the pretext of near-bankruptcy from purchases of silver, U.S. Treasury suspends such purchases. (Actually, the problem was that the paper "Treasury Notes" were displacing silver coins in circulation.)

1894 — Duty of 5 percent imposed on silver entering India. War between China and Japan.

1895 — Speculation in African mines. U.S. currency difficulties.

1896 — Defeat of silver party in U.S. election. Extensive coinage of silver by Russia.

1900 – The United States, following by a quarter-century the lead of the western European nations, formally adopts an exclusive gold standard (rejecting silver), nearly completing the worldwide stage-setting for paper to become the *de facto* world "money" standard. Only Asia, Mexico and a few Central and South American countries still remained open to silver.

1902 – With worldwide demonetization of silver and no industrial demand-base, silver price dips to a new all-time low of 47 cents.

1903 – Large purchases by the Indian government. U.S.A. buying for new Philippine coinage.

1904 – Russo-Japanese War. Monetary reform in Mexico. Buying by Indian government.

1905 – Mexican mints closed to free coinage of silver. End of Russo-Japanese War. Internal troubles in Russia. Continued buying by Indian government.

1906 – Heavy purchases by Indian government. Large exports of dollars from Mexico. Resumption of purchases by U.S. government.

1907 – Cessation of Indian buying. Sharp fall in silver. Financial crisis in U.S.A. Bank rate 7 percent.

1908 – Large gold imports by Paris. General depression of trade. Political unrest in southeastern Europe.

1909 – Some improvement in trade. Good crops in India.

1910 – Death of King Edward VII. Indian import duty on silver increased. Union of South Africa inaugurated.

1911 – Strikes and labor unrest in England. Rebellion in China. Italian war in Tripoli.

1912 — Establishment of provisional government in China. Indian government purchased £6,000,000 of silver in world markets. War between Turkey and Balkan states.

1913 — China loan of £25,000,000. Indian government bought £5,500,000 of silver in world markets. Failure of Indian Specie Bank. Civil war in Mexico.

1914 — Outbreak of World War I and consequent disorganization of money and stock markets. Record coinage of silver. Bank rate reaches 10 percent. Gold standard suspended by warring powers.

1915-16 — Continuation of World War I. Heavy coinage of silver, both at home and abroad.

1916 — Worldwide wartime currency depreciations begin to be reflected in inflated prices, including silver at 65.7 cents (average price).

1917 — Continuation of Great War. The United States declares war against Germany.

1918 — Armistice with enemy countries signed on November 11. Serious political unrest in Russia and Germany. Passage of Pittman Silver Purchase Act, which directed the Bureau of the Mint to melt 350 million already coined silver dollars and to supply the bullion to Britain (for coinage into rupees to purchase war materials in India, where British paper was not acceptable); also authorized Treasury to repurchase an equivalent amount of silver in the open market. Silver prices soar from 75 cents (1917) to $1.02 (1918).

1919 — Peace treaties with central powers signed. High prices of commodities and wide fluctuations in international exchanges. Civil war in Russia continues. General political and labor unrest.

In the inflationary rise of commodity prices, about double, following World War I, silver, reacting to both the general price inflation and the massive Treasury purchases, reached an alltime high of $1.37 in the speculative fever of the post war credit boom.

1920 — British subsidiary coinage reduced to .500 fine. Heavy continental sales of demonetized silver. Value of rupee fixed at 11.30016 grains gold. Worldwide depression in trade. Indian silver import duty remitted. Purchasing power of the 1900 dollar = 40 cents.

1922— Treasury begins reminting silver dollars (to replace those melted three years earlier), for the first time since 1904. Continental sales continue. British Mint commences selling surplus silver from debased coinage. Financial crisis in China. Sales of surplus silver by mint, and continental sales continue. Great increase in Indian demand for gold. German mark completely valueless owing to inflation. Sterling exchange on New York appreciates. Continued depression in trade.

1923-29 — Creation of Federal Reserve. Brokers loans credit boom.

1923 — Mint and continental sales continued. Purchases by U.S. Treasury under Pittman Act completed. Great earthquake in Japan. Political unrest at home and abroad.

1924 — Large continental purchases for coinage.

1925 — Purchasing power of the 1900 dollar = 43 cents. Gold standard suspended in 1914, conditionally restored, i.e., replaced by the so-called "Gold-Exchange" standard. Serious disturbances in China.

1926 — Disturbances in China continue. Coal strike in England, lasting seven months with consequent dislocation of trade. Report of Royal Commission on Indian Currency and Finance published.

1929 — Federal Reserve bust and business depression began.

1930 — Purchasing power of the 1900 dollar = 45 cents.

1932 — Continued depression. High gold price induces sale of gold and sovereigns previously hoarded. Gold exported from India.

1933 — March: Presidential decree closes banks. April: U.S. follows U.K. in abandoning gold standard. Thomas Amendment permits debtor countries to pay U.S. in silver at 50 cents/oz., double current market price. Domestic and world market moving up. Dollar gold price moves up erratically. London Economic Conference Agreement U.S. agrees to purchase its own entire domestic output of silver, as a favor to Bank of England.

1934 — January: Gold nationalized, edict requires all privately held gold to be surrendered to the U.S. Treasury at $20.67 per ounce; gold "officially" repriced at $35 per ounce. Federal Reserve Bank gold reserve requirements set at (a) 25 percent against Federal Reserve Notes; (b) 40 percent against Demand Deposits. June: U.S. Silver Purchase bill authorizes President to "nationalize" silver, requiring all exchange stocks to be turned over to the U.S. Treasury at the decreed price of 50 cents per ounce (14 cents below the U.S. Treasury buying price). N.Y. Commodity Exchange closes silver trading. December: Presidential decree sets Treasury buying price for silver at 64 cents. Silver Purchase Act. Congress gives President unlimited authority to purchase from all comers at any price he chooses; Treasury and private speculative purchases bid price up to 80 cents. Treasury edict taxes domestic silver transactions 50 percent.

1935 — Italo-Abyssinian War. Tension in Europe. Huge purchases of silver in London by U.S. Treasury. Hong Kong and China forced to abandon silver standard. China pegs its dollar to sterling at 1 to 2½. Indian import duty reduced to 2 annas per ounce. Withdrawal of Treasury buying plummets world market price to 45 cents.

1936 – Death of King George V. Devaluation of currencies by "gold bloc" countries. Large shipment of silver to India. Abdication of King Edward VIII. Civil War in Spain. Treasury floors market and continues buying at 45 cents, later at 43 cents.

1937 – Indian import duty raised to 3 annas per ounce. Sino-Japanese War. Chinese government transfers silver reserve, about 270 million ounces, to Hong Kong and later to London.

1938 – Germany annexes Austria, and forces partition of Czechoslovakia. War scare in Europe. Heavy purchases of gold by continental operators.

1939 – German aggression causes successive crises. Germany invades Poland. Great Britain and France declare war on Germany. Russia invades Poland from East. Russia attacks Finland. Treasury buying price of 35 cents, which is the new floor to November 1941.

1940 – Purchasing power of the 1900 dollar = 54 cents.

1941 – Germany attacks Russia. Japan attacks U.S. forces in Pearl Harbor without declaration of war. Great Britain and U.S.A. declare war on Japan. Germany and Italy declare war on U.S.A.

1942 – Anglo-Soviet Treaty. British and U.S. forces land in North Africa. May: Treasury O.P.A. ceiling price raised to 45 cents for foreign silver (restricted to "essential"uses in October 1942 by W.P.B.). October: Treasury O.P.A. ceiling price raised to 71 cents, for domestic silver for "non-essential" domestic uses, as decreed by W.P.B.

1943 – Axis forces surrender in Tunisia. Italy surrenders to Allies and declares war on Germany. Green Act directs

Treasury to sell general fund "seigniorage" (free) silver to U.S. industrial users.

1944 — Allied troops land in France. Meeting of central bankers at Bretton Woods, N.H., forms the International Monetary Fund system.

1945 — Unconditional surrender of all German and Japanese forces ends World War II. W.P.B. removes allocation controls and Treasury O.P.A. raises ceiling price to 71 cents for all silver, foreign and domestic, including Treasury silver. Federal Reserve gold reserve requirement reduced to (a) 25 percent against F.R. Notes; (b) 25 percent against Demand Deposits. Purchasing power of the 1900 dollar = 42 cents.

1946 — Worldwide shortage of food. Shipments of silver to India recommence. Silver coinage demonetized in Great Britain and cupro-nickel substituted. O.P.A. ceiling and Treasury selling price changed to 91 cents, Treasury buying price at 90½ cents. Late '46 O.P.A. ceiling abolished; silver falls.

1947 — Import of silver into India suspended. Partition of India into Dominions of India and Pakistan.

1948 — Political unrest in Europe. British mandate for Palestine ended.

1949 — Pound devalued from $4.03 to $2.80. Communist forces over-run China. Terrorism in Malaya.

1950 — India a Republic. United Nations involved in Korean War. General political unrest. French franc devalued. Canadian dollar floats. Purchasing power of the 1900 dollar = 32 cents.

1951 — Truce talks start in Korea. Anglo-Persian oil dispute. Foreign-exchange market partially reopened in London.

1952—Death of King George VI. Korean War continues.

1953—Armistice signed in Korea. Large amounts of Russian gold and silver consigned to London. Mexican bank puts floor under the silver price by purchases at 86 cents.

1954—London Gold Market reopened, March 22.

1955—Purchasing power of the 1900 dollar = 28 cents.

1956—Britain returns 66 million ounces of lend-lease silver to U.S.A.

1957—All lend-lease silver returned to U.S. European surplus silver sold in London.

1958—Recovery of Sterling. Partial convertibility of Sterling, December 29th.

1959—More countries return to silver coinage. Labor troubles lead to temporary shortage of silver both in the U.S.A. and abroad. U.S. Treasury's "free stock" of silver peaks at 222 million ounces.

1960—Credit squeeze. Congo chaos. Rumors of devaluation of U.S. dollar cause rush of speculative gold buying. Highest quotation over $40 per ounce (October 20). Purchasing power of the 1900 dollar = 26 cents. U.S. Treasury's "free stock" of silver drops to 110 million ounces.

1961—China a large seller of silver. U.S. Treasury stops selling silver to industrial users. Sharp price advances in New York and London. U.S. Treasury controls price in narrow range around 90.5 cents by sales at about 91 cents. November: Treasury suspends sales. Price rapidly raises to $1.05; prior to suspension of sales, Treasury lost 75 percent of its "free reserves." U.S. Treasury's "free stock" of silver drops to 22 million ounces. Administrative order issued replacing $5 and $10 silver certificates with Federal Reserve Notes.

1962—Mexico stops selling silver in New York, September 24. Record high prices for silver in London and New York in October. Price rises to $1.20. U.S. Treasury dips into reserves and loses 96 million troy ounces (77.4 million troy ounces for coinage).

1963—President Kennedy assassinated November 22. U.S. Treasury sells silver at 129.293 cents per ounce. Repeal of Thomas Amendment. New York Commodity Exchange re-establishes trading in silver futures for the first time in 30 years. In Congressional testimony, Secretary Dillon argued that, with the passage of the proposed legislation, the government's silver reserves would "assure an adequate supply of silver to meet our coinage requirements for the next ten to twenty years." June: Price rises to $1.28 per ounce. P.L. 88-36 repeals all silver purchase legislation, "authorizes" President to direct issue of $1 Federal Reserve Notes and specifies continued redemption on demand of silver certificates. September: Price rises to $1.29. First largescale redemption of silver certificates. U.S. Treasury re-enters market, selling to all comers at coinage value of $1.292929292, re-establishing Treasury price control.

1964—New York price unchanged at 129.3 cents. London prices reach new record levels. Great silver rush of '64. The Philadelphia and Denver mints are unable to keep up with the public's burgeoning demand for silver coin. In mid-1964, the Treasury places its two operating mints on a round-the-clock, seven-days-a-week intensified "crash program," in an attempt to double the annual production of coins from four to eight billion in a year's time using all possible equipment and facilities—including the San Francisco Assay Office—and obtains Congressional authorization to continue the 1964 date on new coins indefinitely, so that it could flood the market with 1964 coins and "destroy" incentive for "hoarders" to keep such coins. U.S. Treasury loses 369 million troy ounces (203 million ounces for coinage). Treasury stocks dropped 23 percent in 1964 alone, to 1.2 billion ounces. Federal Reserve gold reserve requirements reduced to (a) 25 percent against Federal Reserve Notes; (b) 0 percent against Demand Deposits.

1965 – Death of Sir Winston Churchill. Rhodesia makes unilateral Declaration of Independence. Heavy sales of U.S. Treasury silver continued. USSR ships nine million ounces of silver to United Kingdom. July: Passage of "Coinage Act of 1965" eliminating U.S. 90 percent silver coins, directing face-saving 40 percent half-dollars and base metal subsidiary coins, reasserting legal tender to Federal Reserve paper for all debts public and private, *authorizing Secretary of the Treasury to limit and/or prohibit trade in or loans on silver coins*, and directing symbol and word "Liberty" and slogan "In God We Trust" be placed on all U.S. coins allows Secretary of Treasury to utilize gain of seigniorage (97 percent), and establishing 15 year imprisonment for non-sanctioned counterfeiting. Established and directed a "Joint Commission on Coinage" to determine ". . . time when . . . the United States should cease to maintain [i.e., control] the price of silver . . ." U.S. Treasury loses 418 million troy ounces (320.3 for coinage). In the five-year period 1961-65 the U.S. Treasury minted 768 million ounces of silver coins, an average of 153 million ounces per year. This was four times the normal rate of coinage, which averaged only 36 million ounces of its precious silver hoard onto world markets, selling to all comers at or below $1.29. Altogether U.S. Treasury silver stocks in these five years dropped over one billion ounces to only 796 million ounces by 1965 yearend. Purchasing power of the 1900 dollar = 32 cents.

1966 – Credit squeeze. Gold in demand. Last full year the U.S. Treasury is able to hold the silver price at the $1.293 coinage value. First year of massive production of cupro-nickel quarters and dimes; also is record year for production of the 40 percent silver Kennedy half and minting of this single silver coin consumes 54 million ounces. Circulating coin shortage is at critical stage. The U.S. Treasury, while publicly moaning about the coin shortage, secretly begins pulling silver coins out of circulation to recover silver for its own use and sales. Officially reported silver stock drops 204 million ounces to 592 million ounces.

1967 — Heavy buying of gold and silver due to currency fears. Sterling under pressure, devalued to $2.40 November 17. Gold in heavy demand November and December. First-quarter average market price $1.293. May 18: U.S. Treasury stops sales at $1.293 to foreign purchasers and to "non-legitimate" domestic buyers. In the next four weeks, London prices move up from $1.30 to $1.75. U.S. silver users scramble for U.S. Treasury silver at $1.293 price. *Treasury edict prohibits melting coins.* June 24: President Johnson signs law authorizing U.S. Treasury to use 150 million ounces from the silver certificate reserve and to default on silver certificate redemptions after June 24, 1968. (Since January 1, U.S. Treasury stocks dropped 150 million ounces.) Second-quarter average market price New York, $1.293, London, $1.45. June 29: In a move to eliminate two-tier silver profits, Indiana Senator Hartke introduces bill to reimpose the silver transfer tax, saying the situation today is similar to the 1930s when ". . . Secretary Morgenthau invoked this transfer tax to prevent 25 or 30 people [sic] from making $25,000,000 to $30,000,000 through a monetary program of the U.S. government." The bill did not pass. July 14: U.S. Treasury stops sales to anyone at the $1.293 "mint price," and announces continued sales to the domestic users through the General Services Administration (GSA) on a "sealed bid" basis will be made at the rate of two million ounces per week at or near world market prices. August 4: First weekly auction of U.S. government silver by the General Services Administration (GSA). Third-quarter average market price $1.67. Purchasing power of the 1900 dollar = 22 cents. October 20: U.S. Treasury announces that it will no longer sell .999 fine silver to U.S. industry because the remaining pure silver is needed for the strategic defense reserve stockpile. Also announces its program of withdrawal of silver coins from circulation, saying that all future GSA sales will be of this lower grade .900 fine metal. Fourth-quarter average market price $1.93. November 19: Great Britain devalues the pound sterling by 17 percent, providing an instant pound sterling profit of 17 percent for sterling area silver owners. December 6: U.S. Treasury announces it is resuming sales of .999 pure silver to U.S. users because .999 silver is essential for industry. U.S. Treasury loses 239 million ounces (44 million ounces for coinage). Officially reported stocks drop to 348 million ounces, not including an estimated 260 million ounces in silver coins and/or coin-melt bars from coins pulled from circulation during the coin shortage period of the preceding two years, but including 165 million ounces yet to be transferred to the strategic defense reserve stockpile.

1968 — Silver prices rise sharply in the first quarter in response to the mounting dollar crisis. First-quarter average price $2.01. March 14: U.S. Treasury loses 450 tons of gold in one day through the International Gold Pool — double the highest previous one-day loss. Gold pool is discontinued and for the first time in history all the world's major central banks in unison (thanks to the International Monetary Fund [IMF]) place a universal embargo on gold, officially announcing that they have "established" a "two tier" gold market. The market price of gold, freed from central bank price control, quickly rises to $42.00 within two months, effectively devaluing the U.S. dollar by 20 percent. Silver price moves up in sympathy with free-market gold. Second-quarter average silver price $2.35. Federal Reserve gold reserve requirements reduced to (a) 0 percent against Federal Reserve Notes; (b) 0 percent against Demand Deposits. U.S. dollar becomes 100 percent a fiat currency, actually redeemable neither domestically nor internationally in gold or silver. June 24: U.S. Treasury halts redemption of Silver Certificates (for most of the first quarter, certificate holders were forced to take substandard .996 and .998 silver and in May and June could only receive .900 coin-melt). August: Treasury announces that the circulation is now supplied with all the cupro-nickel coins it needs and that there is no longer any official reason for the Treasury to continue weekly GSA silver sales. The Treasury nevertheless announced its plans to continue these sales "on into the '70s" — perhaps because of the unadmitted and officially unmentionable historic silver-gold price link, which had forcefully reasserted itself in the preceding six months. Third-quarter average silver price $2.25. October: Silver price declines sharply, apparently influenced by the growing recognition that the Treasury coin hoard, then perhaps 200 million ounces, would in fact make it at least possible for the weekly sales to continue "on into the '70s." (Although the existence of the U.S. Treasury coin-melt program was announced much earlier, its magnitude was not perceived nor its impact felt in the silver markets until after the end of silver certificate redemption in June when the silver price peaked at $2.56; then, at a time when the money crisis was subsiding and the mining strike was settled, it became clear that the U.S. Treasury by its coin-melt program had accumulated an added 200 to 300 million ounces of silver to play with, along with the 183 million ounces of bullion it officially had at the beginning of 1968. Thus equipped in 1968, the U.S. Treasury dumped another 180 million ounces of silver on the market, continued to coin Kennedy halves using 37 million ounces, and ended the year with a total of 215 million ounces [more than was officially reported on hand at the end of 1967!] still available for market manipulation!) Heavy coin melts from England, Canada, Philippines, Australia and Mexico. Early in 1968 it became evident that many private holders of quantities of silver coins—fearful of the melting-ban decreed by the Treasury a year earlier—were unloading their coins to large coin dealers, who weren't afraid of the Treasury ban, and who were happy to buy quantities of silver coins (at a big discount below their melt value, but still at some premium over face value). An efficient black-market developed that resulted in substantial (but obviously unreported) amounts of privately melted coin silver pouring onto foreign silver markets, which, of course, as the flow increased, depressed bullion prices. This process began in late 1967, continued and accelerated throughout 1968 and the first half of 1969—contributing an estimated 20 million ounces in 1967, 40 million ounces of silver to world markets in calendar year 1968 and perhaps 20 million ounces in the first five months of 1969. Purchasing power of the 1900 dollar = 21 cents. Fourth-quarter average silver price $1.98.

1969 — First-quarter average silver price $1.88. May 12: Coinage Commission meets and announces a lifting of the Treasury ban on private coin melting, for the announced purpose of making private coin-melt silver available for industrial use, and simultaneously announces a reduction in the weekly rate of GSA sales from two million ounces to 1½ million ounces, to conserve the remaining Treasury coin-melt stocks and enable the continuation of sales through October 1970. Second-quarter average silver price $1.73. Third quarter: Market price of bulk U.S. silver coins develops nationwide, the coin premium moves up from 1 percent over metal value to 3 percent, private melting of coins slows nearly to a halt. Fourth-quarter average silver price $1.87. Purchasing power of the 1900 dollar = 20 cents. U.S. Treasury sales of coin-melt silver through the weekly GSA sales total 89 million ounces for the year. Treasury uses another 19 million ounces for minting (non-circulating) Kennedy half-dollars, leaving Treasury stocks at year-end at 108 million ounces, of which 64 million ounces was reportedly available for GSA sales in 1970.

1970 — Early in 1970 it was obvious that U.S. Treasury sales through GSA would finally have to be ended sometime in 1970; many assumed it would be early in 1970 as the remaining stock would barely be sufficient for the U.S. government's own needs for a few years. Even so the Treasury blandly announced that GSA sales at the rate of 1½ million ounces per week would be continued through November 10, 1970, that all remaining Treasury silver would be sold excepting only 22 million ounces that was reserved to be used along with 25 million ounces to be transferred from the Strategic Reserve for the minting of the Eisenhower silver dollar. International monetary harmony, low gold price, exceedingly high interest rates, so that money preferred interest yield to silver hoarding. Also, break in stock market affected silver adversely. First-quarter average silver price $1.89. The combination of the prolonged GSA sales and the extraordinarily high interest-rate holding-cost factor discourages long-term holders of silver. The weaker holders sell, depressing prices. Second-quarter average silver price $1.73. Third quarter: The nearness of the coming end of GSA sales fails to generate much enthusiasm, perhaps because of a growing awareness that a substantial portion of the government silver (that sold in excess of the amount needed to meet the production gap) has simply moved into private inventories and will continue to be a drag on user demand, for a time at least, after the weekly GSA sales cease. Third-quarter average silver price $1.77. November 10: GSA weekly sales end on schedule, with a total of 67 million ounces supplied to the market in 1970. Fourth-quarter average silver price $1.71.

1971 — Market failed to rise when Treasury stopped GSA silver sales, November 1970, causing a psychological shock due to unrealized expectations. Silver Users' Association laid down a barrage of adverse propaganda. Federal Reserve System issued new rules: member banks could not use collections of silver coins (et al.) as a part of their reserves, forced heavy liquidation of many huge bank coin holdings. First-quarter average silver price $1.66. Commodity Exchange stocks decline 10 million ounces. May 5: West Germany and the Netherlands decided to float their currencies; their central banks intervene on the market occasionally ("dirty floating"). Second-quarter average silver price $1.67. May 9: Switzerland and Austria revalue by establishing a new gold parity for their currencies (7 percent). Third-quarter average silver price $1.52. August 15: President Nixon suspends the convertibility of the dollar into gold. The dollar floats downward against most other currencies. The Swiss National Bank stops accepting dollars. U.S. price-freeze imposed. Fourth-quarter average silver price $1.34. November: The three-year decline in silver prices (1968-1971) bottoms at $1.28 per ounce, near the mandatory U.S. Treasury buying price of $1.25. December 18: President Nixon announces an 8.6 percent devaluation of the dollar against gold. The parities are realigned. The free fluctuating of the exchange rates, the so-called floating, ends with only Canada continuing to float its dollar. Purchasing power of 1900 dollar = 18 cents.

1972—January gold price soars $5 per ounce to $48. First-quarter average silver price $1.50. April-May: Silver price uptrend begins, reaching $1.60 per ounce. May 2: Sunshine Mine disaster immobilizes 18 percent of U.S. silver mine production. May: Gold reaches $59 per ounce. June: Gold reaches $66 per ounce; formal devaluation of the U.S. dollar, raising the official gold price to $70 or more per ounce appears imminent. June: First printing of *Silver Profits in the Seventies*. August: Silver exempted from price controls.

1973—March: Legislation is proposed to sell 117 million ounces of government stockpile silver. June-August: Second price-freeze imposed. December: Following lifting of the price freeze in August, silver steadily up to new all-time high of $3.28 on December 27.

1974—February: Silver surges to a new record high of $6.70. March: Legislation is proposed to sell 118 million ounces of government stockpile silver. (It fails to pass.) May: Indian government legalizes exports of silver. December: Ban on private ownership of gold is lifted as of December 31. Purchasing power of 1900 dollar = 15 cents.

1975—January: Legislation is proposed to sell 118 million ounces of government stockpile silver; it fails to pass.

1976—Legislation is proposed to sell government stockpile silver; it doesn't pass. Purchasing power of 1900 dollar = 13 cents.

1977—Legislation is proposed to sell government stockpile silver; it doesn't pass.

1978—Legislation is proposed to sell government stockpile silver; it doesn't pass. Purchasing power of 1900 dollar = 11 cents.

1979—Legislation is proposed to sell government stockpile silver; it doesn't pass. August 21: U.S. Treasury halts monthly gold auctions. Silver price at $9.37. September 4: Comex raises silver margin on futures contracts from $1,000 to $3,000 per contract. Silver price at $11.02. September 6: Silver margin raised to $5,000 per contract. Silver price at $11.80. October 25: CBOT invokes temporary emergency powers and sets limit of 600 contracts per account. November 26: Silver price at $16.40.

1980—January 2: Silver price at $30.05. Comex sets limit on number of positions in any one month to 500 contracts per account. January 17: Silver price at $48.80. January 21: Comex raises silver margin requirements to $15,000 per contract and issues edict to accept "liquidation only" orders. March 27: "Silver Thursday." Panic selling in silver. Silver price at $10.80. Legislation is proposed to sell government stockpile silver; it doesn't pass. Purchasing power of 1900 dollar = 8 cents.

1981—July: Legislation is proposed to sell government stockpile silver; it passes—finally! Congress authorizes the sale of 105 million ounces over three years, starting October 1, 1981. 46.5 million ounces are authorized for sale in the first year, an additional 44.6 million in the year beginning October 1, 1982, and 13.9 million the following year. GSA announces that the monthly auctions will be restricted to domestic users only.

APPENDIX C

The Swiss Franc—Best of a Bad Lot

By Christopher P. Weber*

In history Switzerland will have the last word.

— Victor Hugo

Regarded in terms of land mass and population, Switzerland is a tiny nation. Yet, Swiss influence greatly over-reaches her national boundaries. This is particularly true in the financial world, where Switzerland is a giant and a model for others.

The Swiss franc has no peer; it is the king of currencies. At its high in 1978 it had appreciated 282 percent against the dollar, 25 percent against a strong German mark, 18 percent against the wideswinging yen, and over 400 percent against the chronically ill English and Italian currencies.

This superb exhibition of strength stemmed from Switzerland's forebearance in the currency-cheapening techniques of printing-press inflation. They have been the only nation to conscientiously follow a policy of restraint in the past decade. Yet, Switzerland is not an island—foreign trade comprises 35 percent of its GNP, and its government and central bank officials are subject to a degree to some of the same pressures as their counterparts in other nations. Hence, in 1978 reacting to factional complaints about the domestic problems attributed to the near-trebling of the franc (in dollar terms), the officials temporarily adopted a policy of

---

*The background and historical sections of this appendix are based upon the September 1976 issue of *World Market Perspective* (WMP Publishing Company, Box 2289, Winter Park, Florida 32790).

double digit money supply inflation and intervened heavily in the foreign exchange markets in 1978-79, and in part of 1980![1]

The results were two years of increasing price inflation and (in company with record high U.S. interest rates) a 37 percent decline of the Swiss franc (in dollar terms) in 1980-81. The Swiss returned to their normal policies of fiscal and monetary restraint in 1980-81, however, and their domestic price inflation has moderated. The most recent 12-month period reveals a price-inflation rate of a relatively modest 7 percent. This compares with a rate two or three times higher in the other Western industrial nations.

Happily, the Swiss have been able to rein in their monetary inflation without bringing on the unemployment problems which are now looming large in the United States and many other Western nations. While the U.S. has been shocked by a rise in the jobless rate from a persistent 6 percent a few years ago to a persistent 8 percent recently, the Swiss rate has never exceeded one percent. Consequently, the nation is free of labor strife. And interest rates, that sensitive barometer of economic health, are at this writing (Fall 1981) less than half of what they are in the U.S. This is just one of the benefits resulting from conservative official fiscal management.

Not surprisingly, the Swiss enjoy the highest per capita gross national product of any industrialized nation. A 1979 study estimated it at over $11,000; Sweden, Norway and Denmark followed, with the United States fifth at slightly over $8,000. Much of this disparity certainly can be attributed to the 1970s fall of the dollar against the franc, but Switzerland is nonetheless an extremely prosperous nation, with virtually no poverty. Perhaps even more importantly for the future of the Swiss franc, Swiss official gold holdings amount to about 13 ounces for every Swiss citizen. This figure was almost thrice that of second-place Kuwait (4.42 ounces per capita), and is ten times higher than the U.S. per capita amount. U.S. Treasury gold amounts to only 1.29 ounces per person; only 10 percent as much per capita as for the Swiss and eleventh in world ranking.[2]

---

[1]The franc was deliberately inflated to keep it in line with the mark, since Germany is by far Switzerland's largest trading partner. (Not long after, though, Bern found itself with the opposite problem: how to allay the problems of a franc *falling* against the mark.)

[2]*Sources:* Union Bank of Switzerland; International Monetary Fund.

Switzerland's economic strength becomes even more impressive when its many natural limitations are examined. The country is only about half the size of Maine, with nearly one-quarter of it unfit for either cultivation or human habitation. Moreover, with virtually no natural resources, Switzerland must support a population density twice China's and seven times that of the United States.

Yesterday and Today

That the Swiss still enjoy a remarkable degree of privacy, liberty and success in their financial affairs is no accident. Liberty cannot exist without a tolerance for human differences. The Swiss know that a nation which attempts to force its citizenry into a single mold does not long remain free. This tolerance of diversity has marked Switzerland from her beginning. During the Middle Ages, the region now comprising Switzerland, because of its central location, handled east/west and north/south European trade. Thus, the Swiss learned either to discount or respect all the myriad coins, from *grossi* to *scudi*. Turks easily brushed shoulders with Britons; Spaniards with Russians. In many ways, this diversity and tolerance continues today. Switzerland is a multilingual nation. The relatively small population of 6.5 million uses four official languages. German is the mother tongue for 65 percent of the Swiss, French for 18 percent and Italian for 12 percent.[3]

In large part, the diverse cultures within Switzerland have been free from the friction that has marked other multilingual efforts, notably Canada, Yugoslavia and Belgium. Even when the Latin and Germanic European nations were at each other's throats during World War I, the neutral Swiss were divided only as much as Americans are during a Presidential campaign. There were pamphlets and debate, but there was no bloodshed.

Swiss neutrality is an idea long misunderstood outside Switzerland. There is a distinction drawn between moral

---

[3]Romansch, an ancient language partly Italian and partly Latin is the fourth official language, although only one percent of the people speak it.

neutrality and political neutrality. Public and private debate of moral issues is a regular feature of Swiss life. Neutrality is a concept which applies to the state, not to the individual. Swiss political life is very decentralized; the people are more concerned with attending to their own needs than with getting embroiled in someone else's battles. This attitude is reflected in Switzerland's history.

A Short History of Swiss Liberty

Switzerland was born 700 years ago, the only instance out of hundreds of European peasant battles for liberty that resulted in a lasting creation. Importantly, the nation began as an *ad hoc* military alliance, not a political union.

In 1291, what is now Switzerland was part of Austria. It was rocky and poor. The mountainous landscape made large estates and strong political territories impractical. The independent mountaineers, thrown back on their own resources to survive, wanted only to be left alone. When the Austrians tried to tax them, they fought back.

On August 1, 1291, representatives from three cantons, or districts, met to declare their sovereignty from Austria. August 1 is now Swiss Independence Day, and the Pact they made is still the solemnly revered basis of the Swiss constitution; it reads:

> In the Name of God, Amen. WE, the people of Uri, Schwyz, and Unterwalden, considering the evil times that are upon us and the better to protect and defend ourselves, swear upon oath to aid and succor one another mutually with our deeds and counsel, with our strong right arm and earthly goods, with all our might and soul, against each and all who do us hurt and wrong. With one voice do we swear and promise not to tolerate in our valleys the dominion of foreign overlords. None of us shall do harm unto a comrade whether to his body or to his possessions. He amongst us who shall be judged blameworthy shall repair his wrongdoing. Should discord arise between Confederates then shall our elders foregather and act as mediators. This our Covenant is drawn up for the good of all and shall, with God's

help, endure for ever. Delivered in the year of Our Lord one thousand two hundred and ninety one in the beginning of the month of August.

After a century of battle, Switzerland was free. Small bands of Swiss defending their homeland and fighting in guerrilla fashion dealt the invaders one defeat after another. At the battle of Morgarten (1315), 600 Swiss mauled a force of 12,000 Austrian knights, using those guerrilla tactics of decentralization, mobility and surprise that were to be so successful in gaining American independence centuries later. This determined desire for liberty made the name Swiss synonymous with the spirit of revolution. In fact, the very word "Schwyzer" was used then as most people use "anarchist" today. Maximilian of Austria (who lost the cantons) called any of his rebellious subjects, whether Croatian or Bohemian, "Swiss."

For a time after her revolution, Switzerland was the strongest military power in Europe. The nation then briefly succumbed to a program of chauvinistic conquest (at one point making even Milan a satellite), before being defeated in 1515. This put a permanent end to any Swiss dreams of imperialism. Her neutrality was recognized by Europe a century later. Even so, Switzerland was drawn into one last war, this with Napoleon. But even he soon left them alone, and the Swiss have lived in peace and prosperity ever since.

One Government; Many Governments

Switzerland for its first two centuries had neither a capital nor a legal center, and not even a written constitution except the Pact of 1291. (Cantonal delegates met spontaneously in various Swiss cities as the need arose.) There was no true constitution until the Federal one adopted in 1848.

Switzerland's official name is the Confederation of Switzerland. As a confederation, the Swiss still practice a system much like one America once had under the Articles of Confederation, which were unfortunately soon abandoned in favor of the more statist Constitution of 1787. A federation, as the Latin *foedus* tells us, is a sworn alliance among equals.

A confederate system stresses local government. The remote central government is not considered one's "own," and therefore its initiatives stimulate local defenses. At the same time, the central government acts as a counterweight to local despotism. To most Swiss the "State" is cantonal, not federal. And there are 26 cantons in small Switzerland. Cantonal loyalty is high; a man feels himself to be Genevese or Vaudois before he feels himself to be Swiss.

One result of this unique federation is that, while a Swiss may well know who his canton's representatives in Bern are, he will often not know (or care) who happens to be the Swiss President. That gentleman is elected for a strict one-year term by a seven-member Federal council that serves as the actual executive body. These seven are elected by a National Assembly (like the U.S. Congress) made up of a National Council (House of Representatives) with proportional representation, and a Council of States (Senate), with two delegates per canton.

In practice, the Swiss system is the world's most democratic. Every law passed by the National Assembly is subject to popular review if only 30,000 voters request it: less than one percent of the electorate. This has the effect of inhibiting Swiss politicians from bringing to pass harmful schemes. It is a foregone conclusion that most of the new laws subjected to referenda are turned down by a very conservative electorate. Often, laws passed by both Swiss houses of parliament are voted down by the people. And there have been many of these referenda since 1848; they average five per year.

Most of the cantons now have representative bodies, but three of them still operate by a form of direct political participation. They are Appenzell, Glarus and Unterwalden (one of the original cantons). Like the Athenian city-states, and like the New England town meetings, these Swiss cantons are small enough to enjoy this extraordinary practice. Once a year the voters assemble in the public square to vote upon their laws and choose their administrators. This is known as the *Landesgemeinde*. With only four percent of the Swiss population using this ancient custom, the value is more educational than political. From all over Switzerland, fathers bring their children to witness the sight, unique in the annals of modern democracy and unequalled as a lesson in civic freedom.

Each of the other cantons is governed by a Grand Council, perhaps the most important political body in Switzerland as it levies most of the direct taxes. These councils have very close ties to the people: a recent poll shows that most Swiss know their representative on the Council. They are numerous, and *they draw no salary*.

Below the canton is the "commune" (i.e., municipality). These serve as municipal governments. There are over 3,000, some as small as 50 persons, and all but a handful under 10,000. They are almost the ultimate in neighborhood government, and they receive the citizen's closest loyalty. In fact, no Swiss can be a national citizen without first being a citizen of a municipality.

All of this in large part explains a striking fact about Swiss political life. In countries even smaller, a powerful leader has sometimes emerged. There has been none in Switzerland, where the individual retains so much power that no political leader, be he mayor or president, can ever govern by fiat.

A Citizen Army

Although the Swiss army is ten percent of the population and numbers some 600,000, there are only 600 career soldiers. Traditionally in Switzerland, the military is not something to be laughed at, as in France; or feared, as in Germany. It is rather a part of life, and the NATO motto, *vagilia pretium libertatis* (vigilance is the price of liberty) would be better suited to the Swiss.

All men from 20 to 50 regularly devote time to the military,[4] be they peasants or bank presidents. The individual cantons are responsible for raising and training these men. The highest peacetime rank is colonel, and only in a national emergency is a general appointed. There have been only five Swiss generals since 1848.

This is a true citizen army, worthy of Cincinnatus or Washington. An enormous amount of mutual trust must be involved when it is realized that almost every Swiss family has an automatic rifle in the home. (The men keep their weapons throughout their Army service.) The nation is well armed. In 1976, for example, the U.S. sold $450 million worth of military equipment to Switzerland. Only four countries purchased more from America: Saudi Arabia, Iran, Israel and South Korea. The soldiers stay in their own cantons, so in case of an invasion they would have the psychological and tactical advantages of defending, literally, their own homes.

In 1940, encircled by fascism, the Swiss developed a plan to defend their country. In case of invasion, the plan called for destroying every bridge, tunnel and pass leading into Switzerland. Sacrificing half the territory, the Swiss would retreat into the impregnable Gotthard mountains in the heart of Switzerland, and fight on for years. The Nazis, knowing this, left the Swiss alone.

The following excerpt from an article in a Swiss newspaper indicates that the Swiss continue to take a prudent approach to the realities of today's world as they perceive it.

> While many countries have largely given up on civil defence projects, traditionally neutral Switzerland has developed bomb shelters in alpine tunnels and taken other measures in a $2.4 billion program to protect its six million people in the event of nuclear war.
>
> The latest addition is the Sonnenberg superhighway tunnel through the Alps near here. In case of war, four giant steel-and-concrete doors will close, converting the tunnel into the country's largest air-raid shelter.
>
> Defence experts say the program gives Switzerland a greater chance than any other country of surviving a nuclear war.
>
> Right now, 3.2 million people can move to underground blast- and radiation-proof safety. By 1990 not a single resident of the country will have to look in vain for shelter, government officials say.

---

[4]First, all young men serve four months in basic training. In eight of their next twelve years, they spend three weeks in training. From age 32 to 42, the men spend thirteen days out of every two years in training. For the following eight years there is only one thirteen-day period.

About 600 ever-ready underground emergency hospitals are spread around the country, as are command posts and equipment warehouses.

Situated on the edge of this lakeside resort, Sonnenberg is not listed in any tourist guide. But when it was opened to the public for four days on its recent completion, more than 80,000 Swiss inspected it. Among those previously given a separate guided visit was a delegation from China.

In a sense, the above article is reassuring to those who have investments in Switzerland. However, in another sense it is rather scary—do they know something that we don't?

We leave our brief study of Swiss defence preparedness with this famous incident: Shortly before World War I, Kaiser Wilhelm paid an official visit to Switzerland. While assisting at the military maneuvers, he said to one of the soldiers, "You are 500,000, and you shoot well, but if we attack you with a million men, what will you do?" "We will each fire twice," calmly answered the soldier. The Kaiser preferred to pass through Belgium.[5]

The Swiss Spirit

If Switzerland is a unique nation, it is due in large part to the character of its people. The character of the legendary William Tell, "every Swiss' secret hero,"[6] reveals that nature. They are a tough people, and yet deeply humanitarian. It was an "average" Swiss citizen who founded the International Red Cross, which still has its headquarters in Geneva. Many people are active in private charity. In fact, not to be involved in "good works" would be socially damning in the best Swiss circles.

They are a conservative people, deeply rooted in traditions. Sons tend to follow fathers in their professions, and today there's a good chance that, say, the daughters of doctors will go to medical school. So with this, as in other areas, the Swiss do change, while keeping form intact.

---

[5]Roguemont, *The Heart of Europe* (Duell, Sloane & Pearce, N.Y. 1941), p. 190.

[6]T.R. Fehrenbach, *The Swiss Banks*, p. 13.

They are an honest people. The crime rate is one of the lowest anywhere. The honor system is in operation all over Switzerland. For instance, street cars in Zurich don't usually have ticket checkers. One is expected to purchase tickets from a machine at the tram stop and almost everyone does, even though there is only a slim chance of being checked.

As mentioned before, the Swiss labor scene is very placid. There is a virtual absence of strikes. For this, the Swiss are in part indebted to the Peace Agreement of 1937. Signed during the Depression, this remarkable agreement between various branches of Swiss industry promised to waive militant methods in negotiations, and to shun all state intervention. That promise has been kept.

Swiss labor is not cartelized. A result of this is that when prices stop rising, so do union wages. Wages can fall as well as rise, depending on what the cost of living does. It is no wonder that with its relatively stable prices, Swiss labor lacks a strident tone.

Another reason that Switzerland has a peaceful labor scene could be the strong ties that still exist between urban and rural life. The Swiss worker has never been "proletarianized." A number of Swiss industries are located in small communities, where the workers can have gardens or even small farms and vineyards. Even in the largest cities, the country is never very far away.

Recent Economic History

The relative economic liberalism of the nineteenth century world was very favorable to the Swiss economy. There were almost no tariffs, and for a country which must first import the raw materials in order to export the finished product, this lack of trade barriers was vital.

World War I brought economic difficulties, even to the neutral Swiss. Not much trade was going on, but with neutrality the Swiss were a part of what exchange there was.

It was at this time that the Swiss franc and banking system made their first international appeal, because Switzerland had managed to keep both its currency strong and its banks inviolable.

The Great Depression hurt Switzerland much more than either world war. For a nation dependent on free trade, the economic nationalism of the thirties was catastrophic. In recognition of this, a certain shop in Geneva had on display a large map of Europe, the national borders of which were marked by walls whose height was in proportion to the tariff barriers erected by each nation. Every year the walls grew higher and higher, until they almost hid the countries themselves.

But the Swiss pursued a classical liberal economic policy to the last ditch. The inherent conservatism of the Swiss people was never better shown than by their attempt to salvage the gold standard. Most nations followed Britain off gold soon after 1931. Switzerland chose to form the "gold bloc" along with France, Belgium and Holland. Switzerland was later forced off gold, being the last major country to go (1936).

The Banking Code of 1934

Nazi Germany presented a special challenge to the integrity of the Swiss banking system. In fear of having their savings confiscated, many aristocrats, liberals and Jews had sent funds to Switzerland. The German government hit upon a plan to identify these "traitors" and recover the money (mostly gold). Nazi undercover agents were sent to Zurich banks, and confirmed that many of the Germans they suspected did indeed have Swiss bank accounts. They did this by presenting forged letters of proxy in the names of those suspected, requesting either deposit or withdrawal of funds. The banks were placed in a difficult moral position. If they did acknowledge to these third parties that these Germans banked with them, they ran the risk of sentencing their clients to death.

(This was the Nazi penalty for not reporting funds held outside Germany.[7]) On the other hand, the third parties *could* have been truly acting as a bona fide agent of the depositor. To block release of funds in this case could cause financial hardship. This dilemma resulted in the Swiss Banking Code of 1934, which laid down the tenets of strict secrecy and extreme security that still remain intact forty-seven years later.

Bank secrecy had long been a Swiss tradition; the Code enshrined this tradition into penal law and applied it deliberately to all government agents, domestic or foreign.[8] Article 47 contains the heart of the Code: It became a crime for anyone connected with a Swiss bank to violate "the duty of absolute silence in respect to a professional secret." Banking information is defined as "trade secrets," but this definition includes all facts — commercial, financial and industrial — that an owner wishes kept from public knowledge.

The Second World War brought many unprecedented taxes, controls and regulations to Switzerland. But those were unprecedented times; Switzerland was surrounded by fascist-controlled territory until 1944. That they were able to hold out without becoming engulfed by the Axis is a truly heroic tale. But also heartening is the story of how quickly the Swiss threw off those taxes, regulations and controls as soon as the danger had passed. For the first time in years, the Swiss again had a free economy.

One result of this was the low rate of postwar inflation. Throughout the 1950s, the money supply never increased more than one or two percent a year. This low Swiss money inflation rate began to increase around 1960. The reason for this stems from the workings of the international monetary system.

Switzerland and the Bretton Woods System

The world's post-war monetary order, the Bretton Woods system, was based on fixed exchange rates. The U.S. dollar

---

[7]Was this precedent perhaps an inspiration for the recent appearance of the question on U.S. income tax forms concerning foreign accounts?

[8]Neighboring Austria, which also has a long tradition of bank secrecy, adopted a similar Banking Law in 1979. Perhaps, hopefully, others will follow.

Chart I
U.S. Money Supply Vs. Swiss Money Supply

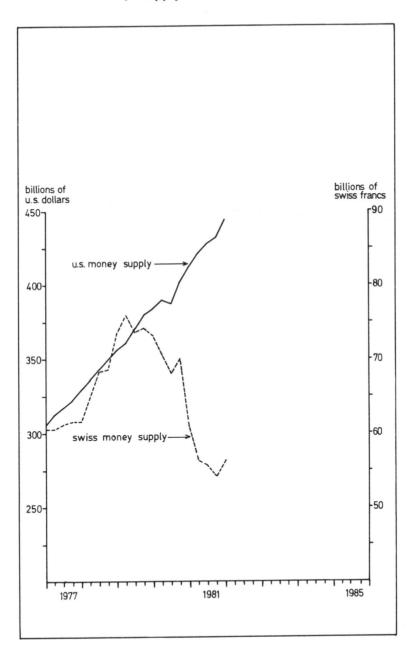

was placed at the center and made "as good as gold." But the dollar *wasn't* gold; it could be printed at will. During the 'fifties, the U.S. inflation rate gained momentum; dollars began to flood the world. Astute observers feared the possibility of a dollar devaluation and saw Switzerland as a money haven. Dollars were changed to francs and put in Swiss banks. Although Switzerland was never a member of the International Monetary fund, the Swiss abided by the Bretton Woods rules. According to these strictures, Switzerland's National Bank was obligated to buy, at a fixed price, all dollars unwanted by Swiss commercial banks. With the increasing supply of dollars, the dollar's price, 4.37 francs per dollar (or 23 cents per franc), became more and more over-valued in relation to more conservatively managed currencies. The German mark, the Dutch guilder and the Swiss franc were undervalued. Thus, the burden of supporting the U.S. dollar fell heavily on the central banks of those three countries.

This burden was onerous. The Swiss had to print francs to pay for the unwanted dollars. While the U.S. gold window was still open the Swiss government could redeem some of these dollars for gold. However, the U.S., in danger of losing its entire official gold holdings, resisted official redemption requests in the early and mid-1960s and effectively suspended convertibility in 1968, doing so formally in 1971. But to their own detriment, the Swiss continued to prop up the value of the dollar repeatedly for yet another year. As a result, the Swiss money supply ballooned, soaring 22 percent in 1971. This was clearly too much. Beginning in 1972, the Swiss froze their domestic inflation rate and kept it down until 1978.[9]

On January 24, 1973, the Swiss stopped supporting the Bretton Woods system altogether. One month later the entire fixed exchange-rate setup collapsed. The time since then has seen an almost steady rise in the franc's value with relatively minor and temporary reversals along the way (see Chart II). In less than a decade, that value almost trebled from 23 cents (1971) to an October 1978 all-time high of 67 cents. It thereafter began a gradual two-year decline to a 1980 low of 58 cents in April, recovered temporarily to the July 1980 peak of 63 cents. It has since declined steadily (as the dollar has strengthened

---

[9] See the opening paragraphs of this Appendix for a reminder of the reasons for the 1978 resurgence of Swiss inflation.

Chart II
Progress of the Swiss Franc vs. the U.S. Dollar

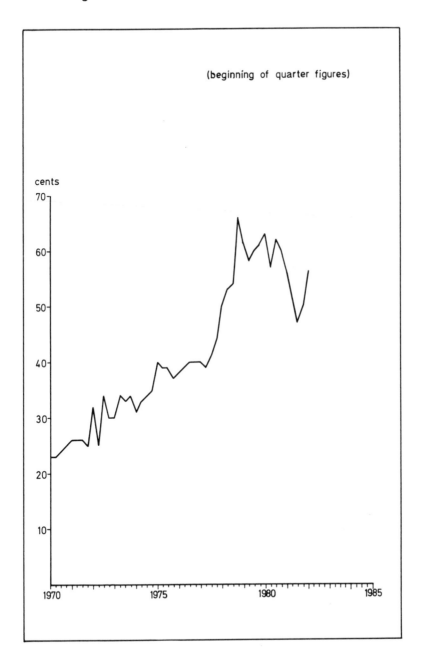

(beginning of quarter figures)

generally) to an August 1981 low of 45 cents. In our judgment this is the 1981 low (and a four-year low).

The highly restrictive monetary policy being pursued by the Swiss National Bank in reaction to accelerating inflation and a weak franc is the single most important factor affecting the Swiss economy. At the end of last year the central bank set a money growth target of only 4%, but growth in 1981 will be lucky to hit zero. As a result, the economy is expected to go through a shallow recession with real gross national product declining modestly well into 1982.

To back up the central bank's tough monetary stance, the government is holding to a tight fiscal policy as well. The public-sector deficit — which includes the federal and local governments — will amount to a mere 1% of GNP in 1981, much less than in other European countries . . . . the authorities mean business. The central bank not only tightened money growth sharply, but it also raised the discount rate three times in the past 18 months, helping push up interest rates.[10]

Conclusion

Quite a lot of negative publicity about the Swiss franc has accompanied the unprecedented strength of the dollar in the past year (1981). The most common point made is that the Swiss franc was still overvalued in 1980 following its mighty 90 percent run-up against the U.S. dollar in the years 1973-78. The main reason for the 1981 weakness of the franc against the U.S. dollar is the extremely high U.S. interest rates versus the extremely low Swiss interest rates. These relatively very low rates made U.S. dollar deposits more and more attractive in the 1979-81 period. However, Swiss interest rates are moving up as this is written and as soon as the present record high

---

[10]*Business Week*, August 3, 1981.

(20% +) U.S. rates pass their peak and begin to decline, which they will in 1982, the dollar will begin a new decline against other, fundamentally stronger currencies and the Swiss franc (fundamentally the strongest) will simultaneously begin a new significant multi-year rise against these same currencies and will rise even more against the dollar. Further, due to events already past, by 1983 a new major international monetary flare-up will once again send flight money into Switzerland, sending the franc sharply higher still.[11]

In the future as in the past we will continue to see hysterical comments by the world press intent on putting down Switzerland, Swiss bank secrecy and the Swiss franc.[12] Most such stories, as in the past, will range from distorted to just not true.

For the individual, Swiss banking offers great flexibility. Swiss banks generally offer a wide range of services not available through North American banks. These services include:

*deposits in any currency;
*the purchase and storage of gold bullion or silver bullion;
*the purchase of stocks and bonds from any country;
*margin accounts and forward contracts.

Dealing with a Swiss bank even by mail can be rather straightforward.

As of this writing, the U.S. and the other western economies are sinking deeper into an inflationary recession. Record high 1981 U.S. interest rates strengthened the dollar against *all* other currencies, including the mighty Swiss franc. However, as the recession deepens private borrowing will decline,

---

[11]It is at such a time that the Swiss officials may repeat their 1978 temporary inflation policy, but not before.

[12]One example was press reporting on the U.S. *Treaty with the Swiss Confederation on Mutual Assistance in Criminal Affairs* which went into effect in 1977. When this treaty was first announced, the press loudly proclaimed that the treaty paved the way for U.S. I.R.S. fishing expeditions for tax evaders hiding behind Swiss bank secrecy. This is just not true.

Switzerland has always cooperated with American authorities in cases where criminal ties led to accounts maintained in Switzerland. This was done even though there was no official agreement. The 1977 agreement, designed to check organized crime, merely formalized what had been practiced in the past.

And the Swiss have wisely insisted that they apply *their own* interpretation in administrating it. Since the banking industry is probably the most influential group in Switzerland, bank privacy as it has long been practiced is likely to continue for the long-range future.

which in turn will cause U.S. interest rates to fall in 1982 and 1983. The Swiss franc will again emerge as an excellent long-term investment at least until 1983, perhaps longer.

No one would suggest that an individual have all his liquid assets invested in Swiss francs or through a Swiss bank, but we do believe that it is prudent and that it will prove to be profitable to develop a long-term program to place some assets abroad. The clear choice of a country is Switzerland and the clear choice of a currency is the Swiss franc.

The choice of a Swiss bank is not so clear-cut simply because there are so many good ones. Ninety-nine percent, at least, are financially sound (just the opposite is true of U.S. banks). The choice therefore pivots on three principal considerations:

(1) Familiarity with North American clients;
(2) Experience and expertise in the investments recommended;
(3) Service.

On these bases, and from personal familiarity we recommend Foreign Commerce Bank, Bellariastrasse 82, 8028 Zurich, Switzerland.

An alternative, for Swiss franc deposit accounts (but not for the other recommendations), for those who wish to avoid the Swiss 30 percent withholding tax on interest earnings is to establish a Swiss franc deposit account in a non-Swiss bank. The only bank we know of where this can be done, which also has the advantage of bank secrecy, is Bankhaus Deak, Rathausstrasse 20, A-1011 Vienna, Austria.

APPENDIX D

U.S. Currency Controls
By Christopher Weber*

> The extent of the control over all life that economic control confers is nowhere better illustrated than in the field of foreign exchange . . . the decisive advance on the path to totalitarianism and the suppression of individual liberty. It is the complete delivery of the individual to the tyranny of the state, the final suppression of all means of escape — not merely for the rich, but for everybody.[1]

Most North Americans either don't know what exchange controls are, or if they do, don't believe such controls could be imposed in their own country. But not only are controls one of the more debilitating of all incursions into economic progress and human freedom, their existence has been the rule rather than the exception for the entire world since at least the days of Plato.

Exchange controls limit the freedom of currency to flow from one nation to another. Often, they are attended by curbs on foreign travel. In extreme cases, travel, currency exchange and foreign bank accounts can be prohibited. While we don't expect imminent enactment of exchange controls, it is vitally important to realize that virtually all governments have used them in the past, and that all have the ability to enact them by executive whim, overnight. The U.S. government certainly has this power, and Washington's use of it would be nothing new. In 1963, John Kennedy proposed the Interest Equalization tax, which imposed a tax of between 15 and 30 percent on

---

*Excerpted from the November 1980 issue of *World Market Perspective* (WMP Publishing Company, Box 2289, Winter Park, Florida 32790).

[1] Friedrich von Hayek, Nobel Laureate (Economics 1974), *The Road to Serfdom* (1944), p. 69.

any American purchasing foreign securities. Interestingly, there was no prior notice of this law. It took the U.S. Congress fourteen months to enact it, but when they did, the tax was made *retroactive* to the day Kennedy proposed it. A "temporary" measure, this odious form of exchange control lasted until 1974.

In 1965, Lyndon Johnson almost achieved a foreign travel tax on U.S. citizens, and Nixon proposed direct travel restrictions. Johnson did achieve a series of direct foreign investment regulations. These were imposed over a New Year's weekend with no prior warning and when business opened on January 2, the machinery — and the people to enforce it — was in place.

Great Britain just last year abolished an exchange control program which had existed since 1939. Among other things, this prohibited foreign bank accounts and investments in foreign markets, and set limits on the amount of money a Briton could take out of the country. A surprisingly large part of the world still has some form of restriction.

Present U.S. Laws

An appendix in Jerome Smith's **previous** book, *The Coming Currency Collapse*, quotes the texts of pertinent laws regulating foreign exchange transactions, and provides advice on how to live with them. We will thus only briefly refer to them here. The oddly named Bank Secrecy Act of 1970 made inroads on an individual's financial privacy. It was this law which required declaration of any import or export of over $5,000 in monetary instruments. Fortunately, an attempt to authorize personal searches on grounds of the vague criterion of "reasonable cause" (from the more strict "probable cause") met with defeat this summer. But the President has the power to institute currency controls overnight, under authority of the Emergency Banking Act of 1933. He could also use the International Emergency Powers Act of 1977, which enables the legal prohibition of all foreign financial transactions and even foreign travel. This was the measure used against Iran.

It is unwise to harbor high hopes that the Reagan Administration will dismantle, or at least not use, these laws. Republicans can get away with abrogations of economic freedom far more easily than Democrats. Remember that it was Richard Nixon, and not Lyndon Johnson or Jimmy Carter, who activated — twice — the only peacetime wage and price controls in U.S. history.

Early Signs

While most governments have the power to impose controls without warning, premonitory signs will give some advance notice. The most obvious is the deluge of money leaving the country, showing up in a deteriorating current account balance. This in turn could be the result of a collapse of the dollar overseas, an OPEC move out of the dollar, a war-ready atmosphere (which we seem to be entering right now), or one effect of a massive monetary inflation to counter a sharp recession. Still other signs are increased public debate over controls and great official concern about "speculators"; increased reporting requirements; and increased customs aggressiveness.

Likely Impact

It is clear that controls would be bad for the dollar's long-term value. This is the story when any nation tries to block its citizens from exchanging the national currency: the world's value on holding that currency falls. Those sectors of the economy which rely on travel and exchange — and their companies' share prices — could well suffer. These include airlines, banks, foreign real estate and export companies.

Acting For Protection

No one can know the precise nature of exchange controls, but one must be prepared for the possibility that controls will involve the repatriation of funds already outside the country. At present, American citizens are legally bound to reveal to American tax authorities the existence of an overseas bank account. So if you simply take money and hide it overseas, you risk becoming, eventually, a lawbreaker.

Fortunately, there are several ways an investor can skirt exchange controls and remain within the law.

American holders of foreign trusts are obliged to fill out a form stating this on their tax returns. Many trusts are "revocable" in nature; that is, governments can call them back. But irrevocable trusts are different, as the name implies. And as Marshall Langer pointed out in a speech given at the New York International Investment Seminar in September, an irrevocable trust which invested in non-income-producing vehicles would be in a particularly fine position: you report of course that you have a trust, but since the trustee can invest in gold, silver or diamonds, which don't produce regular income, you have no income to report. As Langer describes, "You will remain taxable on all the income and gains that are generated by that trust but unless and until you really need the money it is going to sit out there in the trust producing no taxable income." Trusts suit only good-size amounts, since they take $15,000 to set up, with additional upkeep after that, so one should have at least $25,000 to work with.

Foreign Annuities

One other foreign investment certain to escape exchange controls' scope, and one which involves far less money, is foreign annuities, and especially Swiss franc annuities held in Switzerland. Unlike a bank account, an annuity is a *contract,* a long-term commitment whereby the investor pays an insurance company a sum of money now in exchange for the company's guarantee to pay him a fixed regular benefit for the rest of his life. There are annuity programs in every country, but it is obvious that it is best to be repaid in a strong currency: hence the attraction of Swiss franc annuities. They are of two types: immediate and deferred. With an immediate annuity, a single deposit is made now and regular payments begin either three, six or twelve months later, depending on your choice. Deferred annuities can be created by either a lump-sum deposit or in a series of annual deposits. And you can decide at a future date when to receive payments. It is important to realize that immediate annuities cannot be cancelled; deferred annuities, however, with the regular deposits resembling bank accounts, can be cancelled in event of exchange controls. Deferred annuities are a contract cancellable with penalty during the first five years, with no penalty thereafter. More information in this area can be had from International Insurance Specialists, Postbox 949, 1211 Geneva 3, Switzerland.

Other Safe Areas

There are three other investment vehicles which would probably be safe in event of controls. Holdings of actual gold and silver could well escape restrictions. Also, any use of contractual liabilites of corporations to foreign subsidiaries would certainly not be touched. Finally collectibles (e.g., rare coins, antiques, stamps) held overseas would be riskless as well.

Internationalize Yourself

Whatever you decide, though, the time has come to look at the entire world for investment possibilities. Often advantages exist in one country which don't in another. With funds in different countries, an investor's freedom to act in taking advantage of the new opportunities always springing up is greatly increased.

Silver Profits in
the Eighties

These fine books are available:

THE COMING CURRENCY COLLAPSE	($13.95)	by Jerome F. Smith
THE ORATOR	($12.95)	by Peter N. Zarlenga
IMMORTAL LIGHT OF GENIUS	($ 4.95)	by Peter N. Zarlenga
THE WARMONGERS	($14.95)	by Howard Katz
THE PAPER ARISTOCRACY	($ 9.95)	by Howard Katz
HONEST MONEY NOW!	($ 4.95)	by Howard Katz
ENERGY: THE CREATED CRISIS	($12.95)	by Anthony C. Sutton
JUSTICE OR REVOLUTION	($12.95)	by Leslie Snyder
THE ANGLO AMERICAN ESTABLISHMENT	($16.95)	by Carroll Quigley
GOVERNMENT'S MONETARY POWER	($14.95)	by Henry Mark Holzer
THE GOLD CLAUSE	($19.95)	by Henry Mark Holzer
THE SWISS BANKING HANDBOOK	($19.95)	by Robert Roethenmund
WHEN YOUR NAME IS ON THE DOOR	($24.95)	by Earl D. Brodie
THE GREAT DOLLAR DECEPTION	($14.95)	by George Romero
POWER IS OURS	($12.95)	by Gatsha Buthelezi
CONFLICT OF MINDS	($14.95)	by Jordan K. Ngubane
NAMIBIA	($19.95)	by Mbrumba Kerina
SOUTH AFRICA: SHARP DISSECTION	($ 9.95)	by Christiaan Barnard
ASPEN	($34.95)	by The Living Art Company
FACES OF VENUS	($14.95)	by Lucienne M.L. Dewulf
ADVENTURES WITH LIQUEURS	($14.95)	by L. Dewulf & F. Forrestier
IN SEARCH OF LIBERTY	($12.95)	by Frederick Macaskill
RUDEBARBS	($ 4.95)	by Randall Hylkema

These books are available at better bookstores or from BOOKS IN FOCUS, Box 3481, Grand Central Station, New York, N.Y. 10016. Add $1.25 per book for postage and handling. All books are shipped with a 30 day return privilege.